COSMIC JOY
AND
LOCAL PAIN

COSMIC JOY
AND
LOCAL PAIN

Musings of a Mystic Scientist

HAROLD J. MOROWITZ

CHARLES SCRIBNER'S SONS
New York

LIBRARY OF CONGRESS CATALOGING-IN-PUBLICATION DATA

Morowitz, Harold J.
    Cosmic joy and local pain.

        Bibliography: p.
        Includes index.
        1. Science—Philosophy.   2. Religion and
science—1946–   .   I. Title.
Q175.M867   1987   401   86–26020
ISBN 0–684–18443–5

To the students of Pierson College
Classes of 1982, 1983, 1984, 1985, 1986, 1987,
1988, and 1989,
without whose constant concern and attention
this book would have been completed
years earlier

"The only way you can know your limits is to exceed them."

Contents

vii

Contents

Acknowledgments

A book of this nature owes an acknowledgment to everyone whom I've ever engaged in meaningful dialogue. I thank them all most sincerely. Special appreciation is due to the John Simon Guggenheim Memorial Foundation, which facilitates, for so many, the joys of thinking and creating. I want to acknowledge the superb skill of Melody Lane in transforming #2 pencil smudges on yellow-lined paper into crisp, coherent manuscript. Noah and Zach read and reread this entire work and sections thereof and are to be commended for never allowing their critical acumens to be dulled by the force of parental prose. To Michael McClure, mentor in giving life to words, I present a haiku:

> *Pensive spring author*
> *Blessing each blue pencil mark*
> *Petals unfolding.*

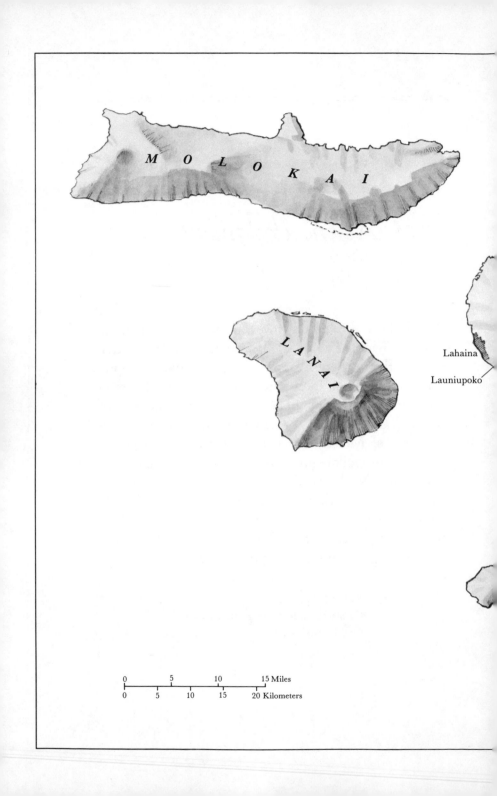

MOLOKAI

LANAI

Lahaina

Launiupoko

0   5   10   15 Miles

0   5   10   15   20 Kilometers

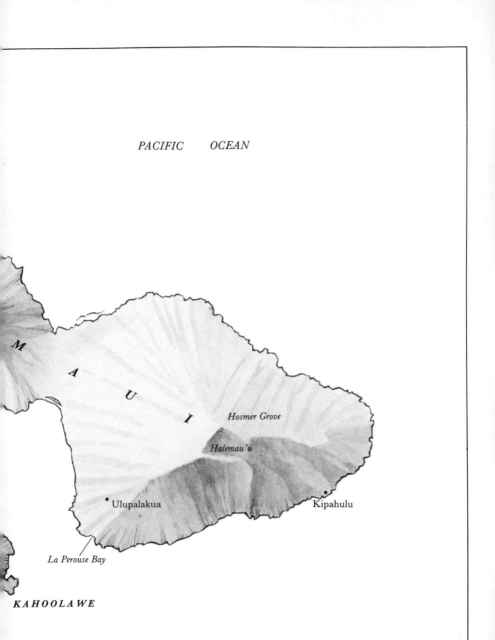

Cosmic Joy
and
Local Pain

CHAPTER 1

Help Wanted: Philosopher

I was a boy reader of the Sunday *New York Times*. Each week I avidly devoured certain sections. At thirteen I regularly took out the classifieds and scanned the Help Wanted columns for entries listed under "Philosopher." After three years of failing that, I absorbed the lesson and rushed off to college to study physics. Along the way I slipped up and drifted toward joblessness, finally getting a bachelor's degree in physics and philosophy, given jointly by the two departments.

My undergraduate years were deepened by courses with extraordinary teachers of philosophy, physics, and the philosophy of science. There was little realization at the time of just how unusual these scholars were, and how fortunate I was to sit in their classes.

After applying to graduate school in philosophy I went off for the summer following the award of the bachelor's degree to earn some money by driving a truck delivering that same *New York Times*. Closeness to all those large bundles of want ads must have gotten to me, and somewhere during July, I traveled the Flying Eagle Busline back to New Haven to try to change graduate school registration from the philosophy department to a biophysics section in the physics department. With trepidation I entered the office of the program head, Professor Ernest C. Pollard, and began haltingly with the proposal that I'd like to study biophysics.

"You'll never make a living at it," shot back Pollard.

"That's a chance I'll have to take" was the best I could come up with.

So I made a living at biophysics and spent the next few decades laboring in the vineyards of science, with a share of vintage years and sour grapes. Then a sabbatical presented a chance to return to philosophical questions and to ask how the scientific developments that have taken place during this century force us to reexamine man and his universe. The pilgrimage led me to Lahaina on the Hawaiian island of Maui. The goal there was to write a book summing up in nontechnical terms my understanding of the activities of our planet.

The route to Hawaii was by way of California and a workshop on global ecology. The first week of meeting was at Mount Calvary, an Anglican monastery in the hills overlooking Santa Barbara. On the third night of the conference, there was a complete eclipse of the moon. A group of scientists sat on the lawn observing the night sky with our monastic leader, Prior Adam.

"Three thousand years ago people in your profession would have been very busy on a night like this," said the prior.

I countered, "Three thousand years ago people in your profession would have been very busy on a night like this."

In one of those moments of truth we looked at each other and realized that three thousand years ago we would have been in the same profession.

The association of monks and ecologists was fruitful, and the Sunday we left, some scientists attended services. The sermon by one of the brothers informed the local folks who came to Mass about the work of global ecologists. He finally came down to "Well, we all have some weeds growing in our souls." Original sin had been joined to environmental sin.

When we got down to the work of the conference, I recalled a previous meeting on global ecology that had generated thoughts about the integrated aspects of all the earth sciences. James Walker, geologist and author of *The Evolution of the Atmosphere*, had pointed out that tectonic activity, the drift of the continents, was necessary to maintain continuous life on earth. The water cycle of evaporation and rainfall drains vital mineral nutrients from the land into the rivers. These minerals eventually end up as precipitates on the ocean floor. If it were not for the ocean bottom being pushed under continents and rising again as volcanoes and mountain uplifts, then the loss of vital elements would lead to the cessation of life. Thinking about Walker's words, I realized the sense in which life is a property of planets, not of organisms. I probably should have concluded that life is a property of universes. That was the unifying thought needed for my project, which was to put together a scientist's world view. The ideas come from the ideologically neutral study of nature, yet have within them a potential impact far beyond the narrow specialties, reaching toward philosophy and religion.

I am not a stranger to philosophical controversy, having appeared in Little Rock, Arkansas, as a professional witness at Scopes II, the creation-evolution trial. My area of expertise was life and the second law of thermodynamics. After three decades of the study of the thermodynamic foundations of biology (a somewhat lonely endeavor), I finally had an audience: Federal Judge John Overton, a packed courtroom, and the press. It was a sobering experience to discuss scientific ideas under an oath to tell the truth, the whole truth, and nothing but the truth, so help me God.

That trial is one of the most exciting events I ever participated in. I was cross-examined for two hours by a State of Arkansas Assistant Attorney General, and I held my own. Indeed, I even felt my testimony lifted a bit of grimness from the event by a certain amount of bantering with my inquisitor. We were clearly "where the action was." And it was pleasing that life and the second law of thermodynamics was of interest to the First District Federal Court in Arkansas.

While the trial proved a clear victory for those who argued for the First Amendment separation of Church and State, it did raise again the question of why fundamentalist Western religion and science have found it so difficult to come to a modus vivendi.

On another occasion I was in a New York law office giving a deposition prior to an upcoming Louisiana trial on the constitutionality of that state's new legislation regarding the teaching of creationism in public schools. A replay of Little Rock was in rehearsal. The questioner was a most perceptive New Orleans attorney whose probing intellect was camouflaged by the friendliest of southern accents. In the midst of a series of queries about thermal physics he suddenly interjected a question.

"What are your religious beliefs?"

I looked to the lawyer sitting next to me, and his silence and facial expression assured me of the legitimacy of the query in cases of this nature. Frankly, I was a bit pained about having, under oath, to discuss something as personal and nebulous as my religious beliefs. But with no choice, I began.

"I come from a certain traditional religious background."

My interrogator interrupted. "No, that's not what I mean. What do you believe?"

There was no escape into the traditional American pigeonholes of Protestant, Catholic, or Jew; this lawyer wanted to know what I really believed, and I had taken my oath to tell the truth very seriously.

"I'm a pantheist in the tradition of Spinoza."

There was a long, long moment of silence. When the questioner began, he utilized his finest Louisiana drawl to stretch out his speaking time as his agile mind whizzed in high gear.

"Wellll, does that mean you're an atheist?"

My reply was rapid. "No, sir, I'm a pantheist!"

The line of questioning changed, and we droned on through the day. The case never came to trial, as the matter was decided on precedent, but I walked away from that deposition pondering my statement.

Pantheism is the doctrine that God and the universe are identical, and this implies a denial of God's having a personality in human terms. I had added "in the tradition of Spinoza" from my memory of Einstein's reply to the question "Do you believe in God?" He had answered, "I believe in the God of Spinoza." If I had been less pressured and had more time for reflection the answer might more accurately have been "I am a pantheist in the tradition of Giordano Bruno," for that martyr of intellect preceded Spinoza. However, since Bruno was burned and Spinoza was excommunicated, either answer seems to have certain classical risks. In any case, Spinoza is closer to my own "traditional background," and he more systematically raised the issues that have been of importance in the creation-evolution controversy.

My first memory of the name Spinoza goes back to childhood even before those *New York Times* want ads. Mother was telling about the owner of a children's clothing store who had once worked in her father's dry-goods market. She recalled that "He used to be quite an intellectual; as a young man he read Spinoza."

Some years later my father recounted some experiences from his youth in Kapulya, a small primitive town in western Russia. He reminisced about the bolder teenagers sneaking out in the woods to read Spinoza. It was hard for me to grasp what could have been so dangerous about the writings of a seventeenth-century Dutch Jewish heretic. The threat must have been obvious to the Jewish community of Amsterdam, who in 1665 excommunicated the man and used the harshest possible language in the official document of condemnation. The danger also could not have eluded the elders of Kapulya around the turn of the century, for why else were the young men forced to study in secret, in the thick woods, surrounded by the local animals?

The next contact came during college days with the purchase of the Modern Library volume *The Philosophy of Spinoza*. That selection from the thinker's chief works, along with the charming introductory essay by Joseph Ratner, finally made clear to me why the gentle "God-intoxicated philosopher" of Amsterdam was viewed with such fear and hatred by the adherents of traditional Western religious faiths. For within his writing lay the groundwork for the structure that could eventually bridge the gulf between science and religion. The solution he offered was heresy, because his god in nature stood in vivid and highlighted contrast to the God in history who had been central to the Judeo-Christian Western religious tradition for the past three thousand years or longer.

The issues raised fermented for two hundred years

and finally burst forth in the fiery battles that followed Darwin's formulation of evolutionary theory. Since that time, the struggle has waxed and waned and has mistakenly been regarded solely as a conflict of science and religion. Within religion it is a difference between pantheists and theists, between deists and theists, between god and God.

The full weight of Spinoza's argument is seen most clearly in his essay "Of Miracles," in which he argues that such occurrences would disprove the existence of God. He writes:

> Now as nothing is true save only by Divine decree, it is plain that the universal laws of Nature are decrees of God following from the necessity and perfection of the Divine nature. Hence, any event happening in nature which contravened Nature's universal laws, would necessarily also contravene the Divine decree, nature, and understanding; or if any one asserted that God acts in contravention to the laws of Nature, he, *ipso facto*, would be compelled to assert that God acted against His own nature—an evident absurdity.
>
> Therefore miracles, in the sense of events contrary to the laws of Nature, so far from demonstrating to us the existence of God, would, on the contrary, lead us to doubt it.

Reading that essay in college changed the world for me. I've been caught in the focus of the Dutch lens grinder–philosopher and his notion that the awesomeness of the universe is the grandeur of god.

Having legally gone on record as a pantheist, I am

free to continue my study, which has as its purposes showing scientifically that life is a planetary or galactic property, and using that result to formulate a world view that recognizes the wisdom, joy, and serenity of the "God-intoxicated" philosopher of Amsterdam.

CHAPTER 2

The Sabbatical Year

As Henry David Thoreau and Gautama Buddha have so forcefully shown by personal example, anyone desiring to face deep and baffling questions had best select a location, take root, and begin. My current locus is a plastic-topped marine dining table in a sailboat tied up in Lahaina Harbor, Hawaii. I am surrounded by a ballast of books and papers, which causes the hull to ride deeper than usual in the buoyant salty water of the Pacific. Some months ago when we were lugging cartons of this reference material to a post office in Berkeley, California, my philosopher-son commented, "Knowledge is dense." Yes, Zach, I agree, knowledge is dense.

Specific questions bring me to this pondering place at this time. The cornucopia of scientific discoveries over the past thirty-five years, added to older knowledge, point to exquisite and delicately balanced interactions between air, water, land, and all living things. These findings have altered and will continue to so change our view of mankind and his planet that I am drawn to ask about their social, philosophical, and religious significance. I want to know what these relationships from the domain of natural science tell us about meaning and value. How can present knowledge about biology, physics, and the earth sciences deepen our understanding of who we are, where we have come from, and whither we are going? I am committed to wrestle with these issues. Like the biblical Jacob one might get lamed in the process, but like Israel one might emerge limping with insight.

Through the front hatch of the sloop I see West Maui Mountains rise a few miles back from the shore. These towers of basalt were shaped by volcanic flows bubbling from deep beneath the waves. Geologists state that the entire Pacific ocean floor is moving as a single gigantic plate that slowly passes over a midocean hot spot. Lava actively rises through this vent and islands appear on the plate directly above the molten channel into the interior. Kauai, Oahu, Molokai, Maui, and finally Hawaii have successively appeared along an arc hundreds of miles in length. Hawaii, the Big Island and newest member of the chain, still adds lava. One can walk on this virgin terra firma, see the bubbling lava, and sense the changing character of the planet.

The peaks of hardened lava shoreward of the ship are counted among the world's land masses, a domain that geologists call the lithosphere. The rock and ore, the crust and minerals, all the solid nonliving parts of the planet's surface are parts of this major compartment. Until a few centuries ago it was universally believed that major land features of the earth were solid and virtually unchanging. But a great age of geological discovery demonstrated the steady erosion due to wind and waves, rain and oxidation. Scientists realized that if this decay had not been countered by processes of buildup, the entire planet would have become flat and structureless eons ago.

As geology matured as a science, more evidence for the changing character of the lithosphere accumulated. The latest example of this dynamism is found in the continents, riding on the backs of bedrock plates that drift on the surface of our spherical planet. These ideas about plate tectonics, and the accompanying recycling of the land itself, must be included in our philosophical views of man and his surroundings. It is quite certain that the mountains I am observing through the raised hatch in the sunlit deck will not persist forever. They arose in a roar of flowing lava and hissing steam and will sink very slowly back into the sea until all that will remain is a coral atoll resembling Midway or Eniwetok. Like organisms, volcanic islands have an allotted life span. They are born, they grow, they mature, they fade away. Before me stands a middle-aged island, clothed in green and bathed in sunlight.

Turning from the bow of the boat to the shaded companionway, I look out on Lahaina Roads, Lanai, and beyond to the great expanses of the Pacific. The ships moored in the roadstead are the successors of earlier vessels that gave this port city its character and traditions.

First were the great carved outrigger canoes that brought the seafaring Polynesians from distant islands to the south and west. Then came heavily loaded merchant-men and aromatic whaling ships, with their polyglot crews of lonely men. In 1843 Herman Melville jumped ship here and spent three months as a harbor rat on these very docks. That fact serves as a reminder that within each of us there is a touch of mad Ahab. We spend part of our lives inexplicably chasing white whales of a real or metaphysical character. Lahaina remains a port of call for searching, nostalgic souls who must on occasion "go down to the seas again."

The ocean stretching out to the horizon and beyond is part of a vast, interconnected layer of brine that covers 70.9 percent of the earth's surface. The seven seas, along with the rivers, lakes, and glaciers, form the second great geological division, the hydrosphere. Thales, who is regarded as the first classical Greek scientist, began philosophy as we know it with the concept that water is the origin of all things, the basic stuff of the universe. For this very versatile substance, in the forms of ice, vapor, and liquid, is the most characteristic component of the planetary surface and the major molecular con-stituent of every living thing. Water is so plentiful that one forgets that it is an extraordinary material whose extreme physical and chemical properties distinguish it from all other compounds. Understanding our planet requires comprehension of the properties of this curious oxide of hydrogen in all its diverse forms.

The most persistent harbor sound is the cacophonous semirhythmic beat of loosely tied halyards slapping against masts. In a twenty-knot wind the intensity of this noise rises, obscuring most other sounds. The vibrating lines are the sonic result of the motion of the invisible geological component, the atmosphere. Surrounding the earth in a gaseous envelope, this geosphere gradually thins out at higher altitudes until it is no more and there is only the vast emptiness of outer space. The presence of an atmosphere on a planet involves a compromise between gravity, which would draw all matter to the solid surface of the earth, and heat energy, which would send all molecules hurtling off into space beyond the planet's reach. On a small celestial body such as the moon, the gravity is weak and no gas molecules are found. On a large, cold planet like Jupiter, escape is impossible and the Jovian atmosphere is largely a sea of primordial hydrogen, which condensed there in the formation of the solar system.

Earth maintains a very delicate balance. Light gases such as hydrogen and helium leak very gradually away, while for most heavier molecules the loss is imperceptibly slow. The composition of the atmosphere has probably evolved over time by outgassing and leakage from the lithosphere. It has moved from an early hydrogen-rich stage to the present state, poor in the lightest element. Thoughts of molecular velocities and gravitational forces come as strange abstractions while listening to the sounds of wind in the rigging.

My movable desk has a special property: it floats on the hydrosphere, it is at the moment tied to the lithosphere, and it is immersed in atmosphere. It interfaces with all three of the earth's major geological compartments. This is the right location to absorb the vibes of the geospheres and focus on their interplay. The intensive scientific study of those relations began in the late 1800s. Geochemistry became a recognized science, and the three main divisions of air, land, and water served to organize collections of data and to classify knowledge. Researchers began to study geochemical processes along with the composition of the geospheres, and it quickly became clear that there was a fourth component whose dynamic action was all out of proportion to its small size. This component, the biosphere, acted as a catalyst for the transfer of matter and energy among the other three. It includes all living material on the planet as well as formerly living matter like sediments and fossil fuels. The coral reefs off these shores are clearly part of the biosphere, but the deep sediments of calcium carbonate from shells is beginning to look like the lithosphere. This is well enough understood as to cause no confusion.

This fourth geosphere surrounds me and includes me, for I am a part of it, as are the coconut-laden palm trees on shore, the sugar fields growing up the slopes, the whales frolicking a few miles out of port, the rotting garbage floating in the harbor, and the middle-aged tourists strolling up and down the weathered dock of this middle-aged island. The biosphere interests me most; for I have long studied how it came to be and in what manner it functions. All philosophical searching has within it, somewhere, a selfish motive to better understand one's self by comprehending the rest of the universe. For me this search for self-knowledge has centered on organisms. Since grammar school a poem of Tennyson's has reverberated in my ears:

Flower in the crannied wall,
I pluck you out of the crannies,
I hold you here, root and all, in my hand,
Little flower—but if I could understand
What you are, root and all, and all in all,
I should know what God and man is.

Existence is so highly interrelated that understanding any part of it leads to enlarged comprehension of the whole. Starting with a specific flower is the poetic clue that we must begin somewhere, and for me the richness and structural beauty of biological molecules has been the origin. But chemistry alone is too limited for the full richness of the world. Wishing now to grasp ideas in a more global context than polymers and cells and tissue, I have come to the geochemist's four spheres as a framework upon which to build an understanding. Such a synthesis involves a body of knowledge vaster by far than that contained in the piles of paper and boxes of books in my cargo.

The lithosphere has been the province of geologists, geophysicists, and geochemists. In fact, any scientist with geo in his title has some contact with the solid parts of the planet. The atmosphere has for many centuries been studied most intensively by meteorologists seeking to develop a predictive science of weather forecasting. In recent years they have been joined by atmospheric physicists and chemists dealing with more specialized aspects of the higher atmospheric layers. The major portions of the hydrosphere are the subject of oceanographers and hydrologists. The study of the biosphere involves a large variety of specialists. Ecologists have the most global perspective, and biophysicists and biochemists are most attuned to the molecular levels. Between these boundary disciplines, the flora, fauna, and microbes are subject to an impressive variety of areas of investigation.

It is humbling for any individual to realize the vast range of materials that must be considered to face global scientific questions, and long ago I made a resolve not to be put off by such feelings. Early in an academic career I considered that broad interests might lead colleagues to view me as a dilettante. On the other hand, there was always the feeling that some of the deepest and most interesting questions lay beyond the reach of flasks and test tubes. The questions could not be answered by the electron microscope because they did not require magnifying our perspective but shrinking it so we could hold in our mind the entire planet or solar system or galaxy or universe. What was required was the mental equivalent of looking through the wrong end of a telescope. One day many years ago I read an essay in which Erwin Schrödinger quoted Ortega y Gasset on "the barbarism of specialization." The words *"la barbarie del'especialización"* in the original Spanish have stuck and have grown in importance. Faced with the contrasting dangers of being a dilettante or a barbarian, I find the choice to be an easy one. Individuals must try to formulate syntheses lest they become lost in an amount of knowledge that is too massive to be digestible. There are not sufficient polymaths for this synthetic work, and Renaissance men dealt only with the limited range of knowledge of the Renaissance. At present there is no choice for ordinary individuals but to move ahead and get on with the work as best they can.

This avoidance of a mea culpa leads to an explanation of how it comes about that I am situated in his particular Polynesian port practicing philosophy without a license. It is in the midst of a sabbatical year, that marvelous academic institution that is designed to allow one to renew oneself in spirit and intellect. A friend outside of academia refers to such activity as "the leisure of the theoried class." In fact the realities of the current scene tend to make sabbaticals a time to generate professional publications. However, I am given to the more traditional interpretation.

The institution of the sabbatical year goes back to the Bible and deals with the concept of resting the soil. It is not well understood how an idea moved from unplowed fields to professors lying fallow, but I certainly endorse the concept. In Leviticus, the sabbatical year is spelled out in the following terms: "Six years you shall sow your field and six years you shall prune your vineyard, and gather in its fruits; but in the seventh year there shall be a sabbath of solemn rest for the land, a sabbath to the Lord: you shall not sow your field or prune your vineyard. What grows of itself in your harvest you shall not reap, and the grapes of your undressed vine you shall not gather; it shall be a year of solemn rest for the land."

In this sabbatical year I have been traveling around the world gathering materials for a study in the history of bioenergetics. After thus sowing fields and pruning vineyards I have come to a point where I will rest from those labors and think about questions that first directed me to the biological sciences. And so I have come to the island of Maui, planted my feet on a rolling deck, and resolved to spend some little time in warding off the barbarism of specialization.

The idea that the earth can be studied in four geospheres came to my attention years ago when first reading the book *Geochemistry* by K. Rankama and T. G. Sahama. On thinking about this material, it was apparent that the lithosphere, atmosphere, biosphere, and hydrosphere bore a striking resemblance to the ancient earth, air, fire, and water of Aristotle. Later readings provided me with convincing evidence that the idea did not originate with Aristotle but probably can be traced back to his predecessor the charismatic Sicilian philosopher Empedocles. Even further study showed that this same fourfold division was found in Brhastati Sūtra, a work of materialist Indian philosophy predating Empedocles by two centuries.

Although three of the geospheres show an almost exact analogy with the ancient doctrine, it takes a little more imagination to identify the biosphere with fire. Some twenty-five hundred years ago, the flames that people knew best came from a chemical combination of atmospheric oxygen with plant materials, such as wood, brush, and olive oil, or animal material, such as tallow and guano. Atmospheric oxygen was a product of biological activities, as were the fuels. The second kind of fire known to the early philosophers was the white-hot sun, which also had a close biological association, for it provides light to drive photosynthetic activity, the primary step for the maintenance of all living systems. A third type of fire known to the Mediterranean world came from volcanoes, which was biological only insofar as it involved the same atmospheric oxygen combining with hot gases of combustible compounds from the earth's mantle. Volcanoes bring us back to thoughts of Empedocles, for legend has it that the great philosopher ended his life by jumping into the fiery crater of Mount Etna in order to prove his divinity.

In spite of Empedocles' final hypothesis, his earlier work rings true. Thus I think of my project as Earth, Air, Fire, and Water to make contact between the classical humanism of the early savant and his Greek followers and the insight of current geochemistry as an example of the scientific enterprise. It has a humane ring to it, and there is the intuitive feel that these studies will end up with a friendly view of the universe.

CHAPTER 3

Evolution and Creation

Who could set oneself down in a new locale without acquiring an unforeseen collection of neighbors? For the self-sufficient Thoreau these associates were the fish, hawks, swallows, and squirrels living around Walden Pond; for me they are the "harbor rats," an unusual group of people working on the boats or around the docks of Lahaina. How very different some of these folks seem from the academic and suburban *New York Times* readers whom I usually meet and sometimes greet.

The first few days in my office in Lahaina Harbor, I am a stranger, and mistaken for a tourist. This results in a certain hustle as the dock hands endeavor to sell me fishing and boating cruises. Harbor rats have a pragmatic view of tourists—roughly, I suspect, the attitude of farmers toward their cows. Eventually, with Lucille handling our social responsibilities, we make friends and come to understand this community better, although it is difficult to think about cosmic problems and be an adequately communicative neighbor. However, after a short time in the floating office, we are established citizens and accepted harbor rats. The sound of a typewriter clacking away from a ship's cabin is unusual enough to create a special status.

Trying to pigeonhole my neighbors recalls Melville's whale classification in the cetology chapter of *Moby Dick*. The standard categories just don't work. Whatever the experts said, Melville was convinced that a whale was a "fish." So it is with some harbor people, neither fully creatures of the land nor of the sea, exemplifying the same ambiguity in classification that Melville faced in characterizing the neighboring humpbacks singing away in their intraisland winter resort.

Americans have traditionally moved from the east, and the pull of the Western Star has often been a measure of a man's or woman's energy or dissatisfaction. When the migrants get to California, they have three choices: settle down, turn back, or go on. Those continuing on may look to Polynesian ports.

> *There's a schooner in the offing*
> *And her topsails shot with fire*
> *And my heart has gone aboard here*
> *To the islands of desire.*

In Hawaii they are met by descendants of equally energetic or dissatisfied individuals who had come from west to east in outrigger canoes or boats of more recent vintage.

The harbor community includes a spectrum of personalities, who defy crude attempts at psychological systematics. If it weren't for my deep commitment to *Cosmic Joy and Local Pain*, I would find it enjoyable to get to know these folks better and to record their stories. Surely several could unfold tales that would reveal much about the human condition. I keep half expecting some wizened old man to tug at my shirt sleeve, hold me with a skinny hand, and begin, "There was a ship."

Well, there was a ship that is central to my search for meaning, but it was not the doomed vessel imagined by Samuel Taylor Coleridge in *The Rime of the Ancient Mariner*; rather, it was the H.M.S. *Beagle*, carrying Charles Darwin on his voyage of discovery. That five-year trip culminated decades later in the publication of *On the Origin of Species* and *The Descent of Man*. These books catalyzed a chain reaction of confrontation between scientists and defenders of the established faiths, which continues with unabated vigor today. These confrontations so dominate the public view of the search for meaning in nature that many equally significant approaches have been lost in the noise and smoke of battle. The argument often lies between those fundamentalists who believe that in a literal reading of the Bible all questions are answered, and those materialist evolutionists who believe that nature proceeds by blind chance devoid of purpose or meaning. How did these extreme views come to be, and how have they managed to drive other more moderate, less dogmatic, more humane outlooks from the center stage?

To clear the air, I'll turn on the bilge blower of frankness, briefly postpone the geospheres, and speak about science and religion. This is not always an easy thing to do on my home turf at a major university, surrounded by scientists, many of whom don't want to hear about metaphysics, or who occasionally express disdain or disbelief regarding meaning in science. Here on the docks it's different; in an idiosyncratic community there's less tendency to stand in judgment of others, and I've had some curious conversations about God and man.

For a start, there is the historical truism that the Western world has been profoundly influenced, indeed totally dominated, by a religious tradition loosely designated as Judeo-Christian, but including Islam. The authors we are likely to read, from the period between 500 C.E. and 1700 C.E., were either within one of these three great traditions or rebelled against them, as in the previously mentioned cases of Giordano Bruno (1548–1600) or Benedict Spinoza (1632–1677). Aside from a few individuals or isolated communities, medieval and Renaissance Europe, Arabia, and North Africa accepted the framework established by the major theological systems.

Western faiths share a common belief in a personal God, and validating claims for contact with the divine is one of the most vital tasks for their adherents. Western religion is thus profoundly historical in outlook. Judaism, Christianity, Islam, and their offshoot sects are critically dependent on reports of certain past events in which the Lord or a representative agent of the Almighty communicated instructions to selected groups or individuals.

These religions are each in possession of documents that record claims of specific interactions between God and man. There is, for the adherents, nothing obscure or hidden about the nature of these contacts; the faiths depend on information being transmitted directly from God or agents of God to flesh-and-blood human beings. The faithful require an accurate historical record of what has happened, for those logs contain the divine word whose truth is not to be questioned. The truth or falsity of the religion depends upon whether these reported interactions with God did or did not occur, as recorded in its holy writings.

The three major traditions are tied to their histories and zealously guard their past records. We often lose sight of the importance of historical criteria in establishing and maintaining those beliefs.

Judaism depends on a real historical Moses, who went up on Mount Sinai to receive the law from God. The documents leave no room for abstractions (Exod. 31:18): "When He finished speaking with him on Mount Sinai, he gave Moses the two tablets of the Pact, stone tablets inscribed with the finger of God."

Traditional Christianity accepts the truth of the Old Testament and adds direct communication of man with God through the Son, Jesus. This religion stands or falls on the historical validity of the Crucifixion and Resurrection. The events are detailed in the Gospels down to the doubter Thomas, who said, "Except I shall see in his hands the print of the nails, and put my finger into the print of the nails, and thrust my hand into his side, I will not believe" (John 20:25). Two verses later Thomas's doubts are satisfied. To understand the importance of the validation, it is necessary to focus on the detail with which the events are described.

In addition to the Bible of the earlier religions, Islam adds a third sacred text, the Koran, or Recitation. To believers, this book is the word of Allah given directly to the prophet Muhammad by the angel Gabriel and set down in canonical form after his death. The Koran shares with its predecessor volumes reports of direct reception of the word of God.

In all cases the times, the places, and the individuals are noted with precision, and accessory details are given to convey the sense of realism associated with the happenings. Either the events occurred as reported, or the bases upon which the respective theologies are founded simply disappear. If one begins to doubt part of the sacred texts, then the entire books somehow come into question. In light of the overtly historical character of belief, it is easy to understand why Western religions have been so conservative in interpretations of their holy writings.

It is not only ancient Western faiths that rely on explicit historical contacts between God and man. A more recent example is the Church of Jesus Christ of the Latter-day Saints (the Mormons). This group bases its existence and doctrine on a historical Joseph Smith's finding golden tablets containing the Book of Mormon, translating them, and faithfully dictating the translation to Oliver Cowdery and Martin Harris. The tablets, according to the Church, were unearthed in Palmyra, New York, in 1827. Either these events occurred as reported, or the entire theological structure built on them crumbles.

Eastern religions, while constituting a complex collection of beliefs, tend to be more independent of historical details. Although adherents revere specific teachers, such as Siddhartha Gautama (Buddhism) or Vardhamāna (Jainism), who were historical personalities, the beliefs in no way depend on the events in which the doctrine was discovered or transmitted. These Oriental religions are a related group of philosophical systems that deal with the ultimate nature of reality or the ultimate unknowability of that reality. Such faiths tend to have a sense of existing outside of time and history. In this regard they stand in sharp contrast to the Judeo-Christian and Islamic traditions.

Given this emphasis on sacred events by the major beliefs of the Western world, we can understand why adherents are so concerned with the absolute truth of the written word. Either their scriptures are absolute and unquestioned, or their claims to God's existence and his relation to them become suspect. Fundamentalism can be seen more clearly and perhaps more sympathetically in terms of this all-or-none choice, which has motivated and continues to motivate many believers.

The Book of Genesis is common to all the major

Occidental religions. It is, on the surface, an account of the origin of the universe, the earth, life, and mankind. For two thousand years it has been the accepted and official version of these events for half the world. To the ultraorthodox of every sect it is correct doctrine, not subject to question. In a different tradition that goes back at least twenty-one hundred years, liberal analysts regard Genesis as an allegory, a divinely inspired poetic attempt of the ancients to understand their world. To the contemporary school of existential theologians, such as Karl Barth, the first book of the Bible is an ineffable divine mystery to be pondered not as science but through the eyes of faith.

The problem that arises from other than fundamentalist approaches is that once one starts splitting basic documents into history, allegory, and mystery, where does it stop? If Genesis is not history, then is Exodus history? If Exodus is not history, then what is the basis of the relation of God to the Jews? If the Old Testament is not history, then what about the New Testament, which relies so heavily on the prophecy of the Old? The whole matter becomes complex and is studied as biblical criticism. The fundamentalists avoid these difficulties by stating that all their Scriptures are true and absolute. Up until the eighteenth century most believers were fundamentalists; the truths of the Bible were axiomatic to the Christians who dominated European civilization.

While religion was deeply immersed in history, early science was less concerned with specific temporal events. Platonic ideals existed outside of ephemeral happenings, as did mathematical truths. The atoms of Democritus were eternal, as were the earth, air, fire, and water of Empedocles. Although most classical thinkers speculated on how the world and life came to be, they were not concerned with dates and time; rather, they focused on processes. For over two thousand years the religious and scientific communities were asking quite different questions, so conflict was minimized.

The modern period of stressed relations between laboratory and cathedral can probably be dated to 1543, with the publication of *On the Revolutions of the Celestial Spheres* by Nicolaus Copernicus (1473–1543), who was both astronomer and theologian, canon of a church in East Prussia. His work, interestingly enough dedicated to Pope Paul III, develops the theory that the sun is the center of the solar system and the earth revolves around it.

The Book of the Genesis is explicit about the earth's being at the hub, leaving all other celestial objects in an accessory role. Since the purpose of biblical creation was man, cosmology was motivated by this view. The celestial mechanics of the Polish cleric were inconsistent in spirit with the biblical view of the universe. The profundity of the difference in outlook cannot be ignored. To believers in the exact word of Genesis, man is the raison d'être of creation, and all the rest of the universe consists of a group of heavenly objects set there by the Creator to decorate the human abode. To today's astrophysicist, earth is but a speck in a vast universe, a planet built out of the debris of a second- or third-generation star. We cannot overstress the extent to which we and our habitat have been cosmically demoted since pre-Copernican days.

By 1616 the heliocentric views of Copernicus were officially denounced by the Church of Rome as dangerous to the faith. Galileo Galilei (1564–1642), the chief astronomer of this time, was summoned to Rome and warned not to uphold or teach the doctrine that the earth orbits the sun. This was not an idle warning, for only sixteen years earlier the visionary Giordano Bruno, another scientist and philosopher, had been executed after being convicted of heresy by the Inquisition. I keep returning to thoughts of Bruno, perhaps as a running reminder of the threat of ideas.

Speaking of heresies, I shall refer to the founder of modern physics as Galilei, in spite of editorial precedents for using his first name, Galileo. Since I cannot bring myself to refer to Bruno and Spinoza as George and Ben, I will not allow the alliteration of Galilei's name to force me into unwarranted familiarity.

Although Galilei was silenced, his views spread and the theory of the motion of the earth around the sun became universally accepted by astronomers. The evidence was so overwhelming that no amount of theological necessity could alter the conclusions. The Church backed off from the controversy; the astronomy of the Book of Genesis was not detailed enough to make it absolutely necessary to reject the new theory, and the issue became moot. The tale did not end, for in 1980 there was stirring within the Church to reverse the heresy conviction of Galilei. Some memories are very long.

The seventeenth century, which began with the writings of Galilei, ended with the works of Newton, the great scientific genius of his time who both discovered the elements of a differential calculus and set down the laws of mechanics in precise form. With his work the laws of physics became recognized as governing vast aspects of the observed world. Sir Isaac, a deeply religious fundamentalist, was worried about those "feigning hypotheses for explaining all things mechanically."

Newton and his scientific colleagues were faced with two conflicting ideas. On the one hand they had, by their own work, shown that the processes by which the earth and solar system function are subject to exacting and unchanging laws. On the other, they believed in an omnipresent, personal, historical God who intervened from time to time in the affairs of men. In thinking about gravity, Newton has a clever compromise: "the hands of God" acting on bodies separated by space. Nevertheless, it is all but impossible to reconcile the law of conservation of angular momentum with the Lord staying the sun in order for Joshua and his troops to continue their battle in the light of day.

This problem of miracles versus laws is not new. What is common to the old convenant is a personal God who interacts with mankind and communicates directly or through angels. Ethics and rules of behavior come directly from the Scriptures; they are God-given. This view came to dominate the Western world.

The original covenant of the Jews appears to have survived the first one thousand years with no record of philosophical question until Athenian philosophy carried by the legions of Alexander of Macedon penetrated the Near East. Aristotle, tutor of Alexander, had formulated a theology based on physics, for Aristotle's god, postulated by reason rather than directly known, was the "unmoved mover," the eternal immaterial source of motion in the universe. Such a concept of god is in radical contrast to the earlier religious view. It is only by convention that the same word is used. The two views of "deity" came into intellectual confrontation under equal terms in the city of Alexandria, where communities of Hebrews and Hellenists lived side by side in relative tranquillity.

The first recorded rationalization of the God of Sinai with the god of Aristotle appears in the work of an Alexandrian Jew, Aristobulus of Paneas, whose writings in the second century B.C.E. used the method of allegory to make the anthropomorphic God of the Old Testament consistent with the god of the Greek philosophers. The most influential synthesis of Hebrew and Greek philosophy was the work of another Alexandrian, Philo Judaeus (20 B.C.E.–40 C.E.). Even though the old covenant held firm from Philo till 1600, there was a constant necessity to assert the dominance of faith (the old covenant) over secular knowledge. This can be seen in the writings of the Arabic philosopher Averroës (Ibn Rushd) (1125–1198). From his work, later Averroists were able to extract the doctrine of double truth, by which contrary doctrines from philosophy and theology were both true. The rediscovery of Greek philosophy by Islamic scholars created dissonance because the mode of knowledge open to philosophy and ultimately to science was different from knowledge by faith, which was, in fact, central to the old covenant. And indeed, it is the fundamental epistemological difference in knowledge by private faith and knowledge by the public methods of science that has been the core of almost a thousand years of conflict. The problem was addressed by Maimonides (1135–1204) within the Jewish tradition, by Saint Thomas Aquinas (1224–1274) within the Christian tradition, and by many others. In every case, the scholars of the Middle Ages turned to knowledge by faith as the ultimate truth.

The beginning of the break with the old covenant in the sixteenth and seventeenth centuries was sharp and at times brutal. It is illustrated in the lives and thoughts of Giordano Bruno, Galilei, and Benedict Spinoza. Bruno's religious beliefs are summarized in the following paragraph from the *Encyclopedia of Philosophy*:

> He conceived of God as the imminent cause or goal of nature, distinct from each finite particular only because he includes them all within his own being. The divine life which informs everything also informs the human mind and soul, and the soul is immortal because it is part of the divine. Since God is not distinct from the world, he can have no particular providential intentions. Since all events are equally ruled by divine law, miracles cannot occur. Whatever happens, happens in accordance with law, and our freedom consists in identifying ourselves with the course of things. The Bible, according to Bruno, insofar as it errs on these points, is simply false.

Galilei dissociated physics and philosophy and developed an independent epistemology of physics. He did not engage in theological discussion, but the Church of Rome was aware of the threat of an independent source of knowledge of the physical universe. After several confrontations with the Inquisitors, Galilei spent the last eight years of his life under house arrest because of his support of the Copernican system of astronomy. In retrospect, the Vatican was perceptive in recognizing the heretical potential of an independent method of exploring man's place in the universe.

Benedict Spinoza, like Bruno and Galilei, paid a price for his philosophical beliefs. He lived under constant threats that his heresies might also be punished by the Christian community. Yet this independent intellectual has come to be known as "the God-intoxicated philosopher of Amsterdam." His heresy was to identify god and nature as being synonymous, thus breaking with the old covenant, which placed God outside of nature. The difference is great, for Spinoza allowed no miracles, which to him would have constituted God's breaking his own laws. Struggling to reconcile god with God, he also regarded the Bible as an allegorical attempt to provide for the common man a truth that could be proved to its metaphysical core only by philosophers.

The towering scientific figure in the seventeenth century was Isaac Newton (1642–1727). He established the laws of motion, which predicted the exact orbits of the planets seen by Kepler many years before. This was a striking example of the exact laws of god as envisioned by Spinoza. Adherents of the old covenant thought Newton's law to be unequivocal demonstrations of their God.

EVOLUTION AND CREATION

Nature and Nature's laws lay hid in night;
God said, Let Newton be! and all was light.
(Alexander Pope, *Epitaphs*)

Newton's colleague, the botanist and theologian John Ray, wrote a book entitled *The Wisdom of God Manifested in the Works of His Creation*. Ray was concerned with a group of followers of René Descartes (1596–1650), whom he classified as "mechanik theists." These natural philosophers argued, in Ray's words, that God "had no more to do than to create Matter, divide *it* into parts, and put it into motion according to some few Laws, and that would of itself produce the World and all Creatures within." The diminished role of God in a world ruled by natural law was clearly a serious problem for seventeenth-century intellectuals.

In Ray's work the controversy about the earth's orbiting the sun, which caused Galilei such grief, is gone and Ray can cheerfully speculate that God might have surrounded other stars by planets inhabited by intelligent beings. Ray believed that the universe is essentially static and relatively new. This is a classical fundamentalist position, which could be maintained without much scientific opposition at the turn of the eighteenth century but was about to become a center of conflict. Another aspect of *The Wisdom of God* is that it introduces in scientific language the argument from design, the idea that God's wisdom (for later authors, God's existence) could be argued from a perfect structure of plants and animals that was precisely matched to their functional requirements.

As the eighteenth century began, an uneasy truce existed between science and religion. Since the philosophy of the day was chiefly concerned with physics, it had not yet come into sharp disagreement with those presumed historical facts that were the basis of validation of God and man.

About one hundred years passed between Newton's *Principia* and the appearance of *Theory of the Earth* by James Hutton. That century saw much data-gathering by geologists. A new world opened to observers who took a fresh look at the lithosphere that surrounded them. Fossils were avidly collected, rocks were classified, strata were identified, and the ground was searched for clues. What became apparent was that the earth was much, much older than the biblical six thousand years, and contrary to John Ray's static conception, the surface of the planet is a very dynamic entity. Hutton advocated uniformitarianism, the theory that geological changes occurred slowly and steadily over long periods of time through processes currently in operation. He assumed that strata of rocks were formed by the gradual deposit of sediment in the ocean; that these strata were compressed and uplifted by geological processes; and that the surface of the earth is constantly being eroded by wind, rain, and living organisms. Hutton proposed a geological cycle that explained many observations. Through his theory, as well as the study of fossils and extinct species, geology was becoming more and more historical, setting it on a collision course with established religions, which by their nature could tolerate no independent challenge to their view of history.

As we look back over the scientific writers of the 1700s and early 1800s, we witness the powerful grip of the biblical version of prehistory on men's minds. The philosopher and historian of science Thomas Kuhn has stressed the sense in which almost all scientists work within some fixed conceptual frameworks and seek answers within these frameworks. Indeed, changes in that structure of understanding are so profound that Kuhn has termed them revolutions. In the period under discussion many of the scientists were trained as clergymen, as, for example, was Darwin. Almost all natural philosophers in both Catholic and Protestant countries had been brought up in societies where the Bible was universally accepted as true. Occasional radicals like Thomas Paine or Voltaire challenged the veracity of the Scriptures, but such individuals were rare. Our contemporaries, no less than the savants of any age, view the world through a set of paradigms that literally comes to them with their mothers' milk (in the United States, they more likely come with some commercial formulation while mothers' milk is being made to cease by some administered drug or hormone). The ideas are reinforced in school and become the prerequisites of a successful career. It is no wonder that they hold us so tightly and often act as blinders to the obvious.

A relevant feature of eighteenth-century science was the small number of professionals and the resulting pursuit of that subject by deeply interested amateurs.

The study of science by individuals from all fields of professional endeavor placed it more firmly within the philosophical domain of the prevailing religious thought of the community.

The half century preceding Darwin's publication of the *Origin of Species* foreshadowed the bomb that was about to burst on Western thinking. A series of books published in the early 1830s illustrates both sides of the emerging issue. *Principles of Geology* by Charles Lyell first appeared in a series between 1830 and 1833. Darwin took one of the volumes with him on the *Beagle* and another was sent to him in South America. Lyell's work established uniformitarianism as the dominant theory of geology and added strong support for the extreme age of the earth. It also summarized the fossil evidence for the extinction of species. The loss of these "created forms" worried theologians, who wondered why an omniscient God would produce organisms unfit to survive in nature. Lyell had written privately, "We shall very soon solve the grand problem, whether the various living organic species come into being gradually and singly in insulated spots, or centers of creation, or in various places at once, and all at the same time. The latter cannot, I am persuaded, be maintained." The master geologist stood on the verge of the theory of biological evolution but hesitated. He had already firmly established the reality of geological evolution.

At the same time as geology was coming of age, the last generation of scientists-clergymen were preparing their finest defense against the forthcoming attack. Eight eminent scientists, four of them clergy, were chosen to write a series of books. These volumes, known as the Bridgewater Treatises, are a grand argument from design based on early nineteenth-century science. These works have now passed into obscurity, but I include a description of them taken from the *Catholic Encyclopedia*:

> These publications derive their origin and their title from the Rev. Francis Henry Egerton, eighth and last Earl of Bridgewater who, dying in the year 1829, directed certain trustees named in his will to invest in the public funds the sum of £8,000, which sum with the accruing dividends was to be held at the disposal of the president, for the time being, of the Royal Society of London to be paid to the person or persons nominated by him. It was directed that those so selected should be appointed to write, print and publish one thousand copies of a work "On the Power, Wisdom and Goodness of God as manifested in the Creation, illustrating such work by all reasonable arguments, as for instance, the variety and formation of God's creatures, in the animal, vegetable, and mineral kingdoms; the effect of digestion and thereby of conversion; the construction of the hand of man and an infinite variety of other arguments; as also by the discoveries ancient and modern in arts, sciences, and the whole extent of modern literature."

The problem with this genre of literature is that scientific arguments from design may be offered in support of a deistic God but do not of necessity support the God of the Church of England, who can only be known historically through personal contacts. The authors of the Bridgewater Treatises were, in a sense, establishing the basis for the breakdown of fundamentalist theology, even though they were doing it in the name of that doctrine.

With the publication of the *Origin of Species* in 1859 and the *Descent of Man* in 1871, the geological and biological sciences became fully historical and were brought into direct confrontation with the religious establishment on every issue covered in the Book of Genesis. The response to Darwinism on the part of theologians and their followers was immediate and violent. Even the word "Darwinism" was an attempt to ascribe a general scientific development to an individual and thus make it easier to attack. The arguments of the mid-1800s went deeper than any previous conflicts, for they came to the central issue, man himself.

The prevailing doctrine for thousands of years had focused on Adam and his descendants as the very reason why God had formed the universe. Man had been especially created, apart from all other things, and thus existed, in his own thinking, outside of nature. With the theory of evolution humans lost their special status; they were primates descended from nonhuman primates and were part of the accidental spawning of species by which nature blindly proceeded. The assault on the collective human ego structure can hardly be conceived. A morality and social order that had been perennially based on a relation to the angels now had to seek its basis for a group of hairless apes. There seems little doubt that many of the deep human social problems of the twentieth century stem from that loss of special status, along with the responsibility that accompanied that position.

The struggles of the second half of the nineteenth century were not between science and religion in any abstract sense. Buddhists, for example, would have been totally unconcerned about the age of the earth; they had already conceptualized vaster eons. The battles were between religions that required the personal historical God of the Bible and sciences that had developed independent methods of reading history. The conflicts were inevitable because the truths of religion were tied to the same observed world as the data of science. There was little room for compromise between disciplines that both investigated the domain of history and came to totally different conclusions.

The problems for theologians were threefold. First, the massive amounts of data from geology and biology created a version of reality that was in total conflict with Genesis on the age of the earth, the origin of life, the origin of species, and lastly, the origin of man. Part of the sacred writings had been declared false by an independent and very successful branch of human learning. Second, the special place of man had been reduced to that of another animal species. Third, the day-to-day role of God had been diminished by the acceptance of natural law as governing all phenomena. With this change, traditional Western morality lost its strongest foundation stone.

I think that there has been a tendency to judge Darwin's critics too harshly. If they stood in the way of truth, as they did, they were in part motivated by a sense of losing the social responsibility of God-fearing men and women. In terms of that triad of values, the good, the true, and the beautiful, they may have been willing to sacrifice the true for what they believed was the good. That choice is plagued with far more difficulties than many scientists have been willing to admit. The theologians did not put the argument in these terms; they sought independent truths with different methodological bases. The problem of truth and how to establish it is one that must be constantly faced in a search for meaning within natural philosophy.

CHAPTER 4

Knowing and Guessing

When Buddha decided to sit under an assattha fig tree to await enlightenment, he fortunately chose a site that requires little maintenance other than the occasional clearing of leaves. A boat is a more troublesome spot in which to think, for it must be maintained against corrosion, decay, and all of those other degradative forces of nature that scientists choose to lump under the second law of thermodynamics. That great empirical law states that a system left to itself will tend toward a maximum state of molecular disorder. Buddha, too, drew some profound lessons from the impermanence of material things.

When I occupied my new floating office, certain defects in the wiring were apparent; a nonoperative blower, lights that didn't work, and a draining battery. Although I had no knowledge of marine electrical systems, I went at the problems with firm confidence in Ohm's law (the voltage is the product of the current multiplied by the resistance) and more generally in Maxwell's laws of electromagnetism. My mentor in marine repairs, Captain Bobbie, also assumed the laws of electricity but adopted a much more intuitive approach to locating problems. If I were a religious fundamentalist, I would assume that the electrical wiring on board was designed by a fallen angel, for my rational attempts to locate the problems were often totally frustrated. Bobbie's intuitive attempts had a higher batting average.

Concern with how one establishes what is true brings me to the theory of knowledge. The search for meaning involves digging into the question of "how do we know the things that we know?" This question has occupied generations of philosophers ever since Socrates first asked Theaetetus, "What is knowledge?" Descartes, Leibnitz, Locke, Berkeley, Hume, and Kant are among the thinkers associated with this search for understanding.

If I take a less than academic approach to the theory of knowledge, it is because much of my recent thinking on the subject was done with my nose up against the oily motor block as I tried to loosen frozen nuts and bolts. Included in the maintenance tasks was extracting the engine for repair and then remounting it. When it was reassembled, all the parts were used except for one leftover cotter pin, which also suggested troublesome issues. In the oily hold of a boat, questions are less abstract than in the groves of academe, but a true philosophy must satisfy both ways of thinking.

A few words must be said for the engine, an Atomic 4. First, it weighs three hundred pounds, a fact attested to by each and every one of my creaking vertebrae. It is one of those pieces of machinery simple enough to be known tactually as well as intellectually. Future engines will conceal many operational steps in circuits engraved on silicon chips, and their essences will be less accessible to direct encounter. Semiconductors are altering our mind-set in ways diffiult to predict. Each technological innovation changes our way of thinking; that is the thrust of Marshall McLuhan's statement "the Medium is the Message." Retrospectively, I'm glad to have interacted so tangibly with the satanical electrical system. As starvation is supposed to be good for artists, so engine repair must be good for philosophers.

Theory of knowlege at its most abstract level deals with a real world out there independent of our minds. It inquires how we know the existence of physical objects, flora, fauna, and other people. Another area of interest is how we know when we are dreaming or hallucinating as contrasted to when we are experiencing normal sense inputs. These odd questions have absorbed some of the great minds of all time. In the end there is surprisingly little agreement among the experts.

Occasionally I meet someone at a social occasion who gives me a minilecture on nutrition and tells me something in the following form: "The healthiest possible diet consists of alfalfa sprouts, brown rice, yogurt, bananas, and duck eggs." The question I immediately want to raise is "How do you know that statement is true?" Why, just the other day I was sipping a beer at the Lahaina Yacht Club when the man at the next stool drew out a set of plans by which he will build a carburetor to increase the gas mileage of his Chevrolet from 24 to more than 200 miles per gallon. My faith in the laws of thermodynamics prompted me to ask, "How do you know?" but I refrained. Theory of knowledge, like politics and religion, is most likely unfit conversation for a sunlit seaside bar.

A thought exercise consists of trying to figure out just how one would determine the validity of various statements. Here are a few of my favorites:

> *This stock will double in value in six months.*
> *Bran flakes prevent cancer.*
> *Astrology works.*
> *This detergent will get your clothes whiter than white.*
> *This car was only driven to church on Sundays by a little old lady.*
> *The earth is round.*
> *"God's in his heaven—All's right with the world."*

Each day we are subject to a range of propositions, and the conduct of our lives depends on classifying each such statement as true, false, or indeterminate (with gradations such as possible, probably true, etc.). Who can avoid having criteria for assessment of validation? Everyone practices a theory of knowledge, or epistemology, whether or not he chooses to think about it.

One problem of modern education is its failure to teach one how to evaluate information. We rely on the authority of teachers and textbooks and discourage students from challenging statements on epistemological grounds. Think how different our society would be if most high school students were prepared to analyze the meaning and validity of the kinds of statements listed above. Problems of knowledge and validation of knowledge in science and religion are so different and subtle that they might be illuminated by a pair of anecdotes.

Many years ago two old friends met at a regional trade fair in Poland. Yussel the Red Beard and Moishe the Skeptic had not seen each other since the former had moved to a neighboring town some three years previously. The man with the long, thick red hair had joined the Chasidim and was eager to inform his old companion about the marvelous deeds of his rabbi. "Did you know," said Yussel, "that my rabbi talks directly to God?" "How do you know?" shot back the skeptic sharply. "Why, he tells me so," said the Chasid with reassurance. "How do you know he tells the truth?" Yussel looked at his friend quizzically and somewhat hurt. "Moishe, do you think that a man who talks to God would lie?"

An anthropologist visited a New Mexican pueblo during a rain dance. He asked the chief, "Why do you dance?" The Indian replied, "If we dance long enough and hard enough, it will begin to rain." The questioning continued. "How do you know?" "It has happened as far back as our people can remember. The dance has always brought rain. Sometimes it takes a day, sometimes a week. Once my great-grandfather told me it took seventeen moons, but always the dance has brought rain."

Scientists function within their specialties without having to give much thought to philosophical questions about validation and knowledge. These are part of the foundations of their areas of expertise and can be used without further analysis. One doesn't have to know solid-state physics in order to use a TV set or a word processor; those features are built in. The conceptual frameworks within which groups of scientists work have been called paradigms by Thomas Kuhn. He asserts that normal science consists of working out problems within one of these schemes. This does not require constantly questioning the fundamentals of the various disciplines and leaves the practitioners free to work out the detailed structures.

A few scientists and philosophers have made a special study of the philosophy of science and provide insights into how knowledge is arrived at. My favorite author in these foundation areas is a former teacher, Henry Margenau, whose book *The Nature of Physical Reality* contains a detailed analysis of how the physical sciences proceed. I believe that his reasoning applies to historical sciences like geology and biology as well, although we want to be aware of possible differences in approach.

For every field of science the starting points are the phenomena, observations made by interested and curious individuals. These raw materials may be classified as sense data: sights, sounds, tactile sensations, and the like. There is a question as to whether we ever experience pure sensations or whether there is an act of interpretation in every act of sensing. For empiricists such as the English philosopher John Locke, the sense data are the primary facts. For Immanuel Kant and his followers there are necessary truths prior to experience that are inherent in the structure of our minds and are thus imposed on experience, influencing the nature of that experience. All issues about the character of our input data are not fully resolved, but there is general agreement that such data are the starting points of science.

Using these sense data, we develop theoretical notions, which Professor Margenau calls constructs. The simplest kinds of constructs include the assertion of the existence of material objects. We start from inputs like bright green, rectangular, and heavy, and then conceptually arrive at the existence of an object, in this case a book sitting on my table getting stained by coffee that has just spilled. This notion of things is such a familiar abstraction that we rarely think about it very much, yet it is the first step in formulating a scientific view.

From concrete entities we move to more abstract ideas, such as relations between objects. This generates new constructs such as space, impenetrability, and gravity. These constructs and the ways they relate to one another become the theories of science. Theories always involve postulating something that we don't know directly from sense data that are immediately apprehended. Without this kind of analysis experience would be an unorganized collection of sensations. Much impressionistic modern art has something of this character; it is perhaps as close as we come to pure sensations uninfluenced by theory.

Of all the possible theories and constructs that can be thought of, only a certain very limited class are of interest to science, which is concerned with those ideas that can be related back to the observed world of sense

data or experimental findings. This path from percep-
tions (sense data) to constructs and back to sense data
is called the loop of verification, and is an essential
feature of all science. For example, there is no voltage at
my blower motor. Using a large number of constructs of
electrical theory, I postulate that there is a break in the
wiring circuit. I go back to the world of sense data and
find a place in the ground circuit where a wire has come
loose from the engine block.

To persist in science, a theory must survive the loop
of verification, for if it predicts something contrary to
what we observe, it is false and must be rejected on
logical grounds. If it can't be related to observations because it doesn't contain a full loop back to sense data, it
is rejected as not dealing with the real world. Philosopher of science Karl Popper says that falsification is the
major criterion for ascertaining the invalidity of a scientific idea. As long as a theory survives without being
falsified, it is, according to Popper, tentatively valid,
and this kind of validity, in his view, is as well as we
can ever do. Failure to falsify, however, doesn't guarantee the truth of a theory. I postulate that if the moon
is made of green cheese, it will reflect yellow light. I go
back to the world of sense data, and sure enough, the
moon reflects yellow light. My theory tentatively survives, even though in this case it is patently wrong. I
could go on: If the moon is made of green cheese, it
will have a density of less than 1.5. By a very elaborate
series of operations involving Newton's laws of motion
I go back to the world of sense data and find the density
far in excess of 1.5. I conclude the theory that the moon

is made of green cheese is wrong. No amount of verification guarantees that a theory is right (we may not have asked the proper questions), but a single case of falsification is sufficient to reject a theory.

All science is tentative; any aspect constantly stands poised on the verge of being rejected by new observations. In the abstract, this would be accepted by almost all scientists, but it is not quite the way things actually work. Continued verification of a theory when subjected to a great number of tests of different types lends confidence that it will never be falsified in the future. As a psychological matter, some constructs become more and more entrenched with continued loops of verification. However, a theory is only a theory, and if we refuse to admit—in principle—vulnerability to new observations, then it ceases to be a theory and becomes a dogma.

One additional aspect of science must be stressed: It is a public social activity. All observations must be available to anyone wishing to carry out the procedures. Esoteric knowledge cannot be admitted. All experiments and observations must be subject to independent repetition by others. Similarly, the theoretical operations linking constructs, the formal, logical, and mathematical steps, must be universally accessible. Although Bobbie and I may disagree as to where the short circuit is, the ohmmeter reading is accessible to both of us, and the wrong theory can eventually be eliminated by falsification.

When conceptual disputes arise in science, they are tentatively resolved by a vote of the participants. This is not a formal procedure, and minority opinions may persist and eventually become accepted. Although mistakes may be made in this way, the public character of the enterprise allows the mistakes to be rectified by new voters or by old voters who change their minds. As a matter of historical record, many scientists have changed their minds on major issues.

We have left out one difficult issue. Among the enormous number of possible theories that are subject to the loop of vertification, how do we select the "right ones"? How do we choose one theory or set of constructs over another when neither is falsified by the data? On that issue Margenau has carefully examined the way in which physics has developed and has arrived at the conclusion that there are a number of independent criteria by which theories are judged. He calls these metaphysical criteria, to stress the fact that they lie outside of the theories themselves and therefore are metarules of operation. To realize that we require metaphysical assessment is to face up to the fact that science cannot be done, as the logical positivists have maintained, in the total absence of philosophical bias. Rather than trying to be purer than pure, we have to concede that part of our own mind-set is being imposed on the way we structure the subject. This may not be the most pristine approach, but it is probably the most realistic one. It recognizes what has been done. Since physics succeeds so well, we are inclined to use its theory of knowledge as a model for the philosophy of all science.

Among the criteria discussed in Margenau's *Nature of Physical Reality* are simplicity, connectedness, causality, and elegance. *Simplicity* is a device for unburdening the human mind. If we have two theories equally effective in verification and equal by other criteria, we pick the simpler of the two. This approach goes back at least to the fourteenth-century English philosopher William of Occam and in its classical form is known as Occam's razor (cut out the extraneous). It seems rather obvious and indeed it is; nevertheless there have been systems of human thought that introduced multiple explanations and esoteric complexity. This is not the way of science. In spite of technical jargon and elaborate mathematics that often bewilder the layman, the physicist is always proceeding as simply as possible toward the solution of a given problem.

Connectivity is less obvious when viewed from outside science, but is well known to practitioners in all branches. Science is not a set of isolated theories to handle independently different classes of data; rather, it involves a highly interconnected group of ideas. Discoveries in one domain insistently affect others. Concepts such as the atomic theory and the periodic table apply in every branch of natural philosophy. The connectivity criteria lead to choosing theories on the basis of the number of contacts they make with constructs in all domains of science. Part of the great power and beauty of physics is that it all fits together at a conceptual and explanatory level. The same quantum mechanics that gives us information from the spectra of stars tells us about the chemical bonding forces within living cells. The gravitational theory that describes the orbits of planets predicts the change of pressure with height in the earth's atmosphere. Thermodynamics applies to both muscles and nuclear power plants. I personally find this connectedness one of the most persuasive arguments for the extent to which science has given us insight in understanding the world.

Causality, the doctrine of cause and effect, is not an empirical fact, as philosopher David Hume showed so vividly two hundred years ago. Event A may invariably be associated with event B, but to state that A is the cause of B involves an independent metaphysical assumption about the nature of the world. We are so used to thinking in terms of causal relations in science that we often lose sight of the necessity of explicitly understanding the character of theories. Margenau finds causality one of the necessary criteria for developing science in its present format. Given our choice of theories, we opt for the one that provides causal relations between constructs.

Criteria of *elegance* are even harder to define, but not infrequently a theoretical physicist will recognize a theory of choice by its beauty. There is a style to science. Within the limits posed by verification and falsification, style can play a role in how one conceptualizes the world.

Science is not a pursuit free of philosophical assumptions. On the contrary, it is imbued with metaphysical overviews, a fact that many researchers would prefer kept in the closet. Any discipline that seeks knowledge of the world must develop an epistemology and a corresponding set of metaphysical prerequisites. Before we look at some corresponding features of various modes of religious thought, the question that emerges is why the approach of science has been so successful in gaining the attention and confidence of so large a segment of the public, in spite of most people's lack of understanding of the basic theories.

I believe that the answer to that question is largely pragmatic; science works with great success in an engineering sense. It was Darwin's good fortune to write the *Origin of Species* during the days of the Industrial Revolution. The technological results of natural philosophy were affecting people's lives in profound ways. Since almost everyone benefited by this technology, most individuals were sympathetic to the mode of thought that lay behind it. Subsequently, there has been an ever-increasing impact on daily life due to advances in medicine, agriculture, and engineering, all of which have been based on scientific methods. Today we are tempted to ask, Can a technique of knowledge that flies me across the country in a 747 and softly sets me down at my destination be other than correct? If science is not doing a good job about understanding the real world, how can it be doing such an outstanding job of manipulating that world? At the core of our acceptance of science is the power it gives in a material sense. That use of science is so much a part of our lives that its basic validity is unquestioned. The most ardent fundamentalist does not reject the technological fruits of physics, chemistry, and biology.

Religion presents a much older, more complicated, and more difficult epistemological study. There is such a variety of ways of obtaining and evaluating knowledge that they are difficult to systematize.

In Western theology, as we have noted, the primary source of knowledge is revelation. An individual or individuals report a direct experience of contact with a personal God who conveys a message. These experiences have a private character and cannot be reproduced at will by others, as is the case in science. Hence, each report raises such questions as:

Is the individual telling the truth?
Was the experience a hallucination?
Was the experience a dream?

There are criteria for separating deception, fraud, and delusion from a "true" experience, but they are not absolute. We have no objective method of knowing that an experience has taken place. This is one of the major differences between science, where laboratory experiments can be repeated endlessly, and religious experiences, which are presumed to be unique.

After "revelations" take place, they are incorporated in sacred documents. This raises the further issues of whether the events were properly reported and transmitted and whether we understand the meaning of the report, which may be in an unfamiliar language. This kind of study, which has been termed biblical exegesis, or higher criticism, places the responsibility of interpreting the "word" in the hands of scholars, who often can reach no consensus. If the students of scripture begin to use the methods of science to evaluate their documents, they open themselves to accepting the conclusions of science wherever they may lead. A living religion must have leaders who interpret the scriptures to the faithful. These interpretations may change with time, and the primary data of revealed religions are not public, therefore the adherents need epistemological approaches different from those of natural philosophy.

A second approach, religious existentialism, starts by denying the possibility of resolving the epistemological problem and makes a leap of faith to the acceptance of a personal God and the authenticity of certain scriptures. This approach requires no validation for the believers, since such problems have been leaped over. The sacred documents are also to be understood by faith. Again we note the private rather than public nature of such an approach. It has led people to a whole series of unrelated beliefs and allows no method of choosing between them to arrive at a more public formulation.

A third group attempts to deduce the existence and nature of God from philosophical arguments. This tradition, already discussed a bit, exists within Western religion, which tries to bolster the directly perceived deity of revelation with a series of arguments showing the logical or metaphysical necessity of such a presence. The arguments are associated with Aristotle, Saint Augustine, Saint Anselm, and Saint Thomas Aquinas, as well as with others inside and outside the Church. The problem that emerges is that the philosopher's God may be very different from the scriptural God. When this postulation of a God is carried out independently of any scriptural roots, it is called deism, a view of religion that has many followers. For the Church Fathers and modern scholars who try to develop support for a historical God by abstract intellectual arguments, the path is a difficult one. Intellectual arguments may support or refute the God of history. Recognizing the validity of such an approach in theology opens up the outcome to both possibilities. Indeed, the existence of such arguments within religion made it easier to confront theology with the conclusions of science.

As one gets further and further from Bible-based theology, the meaning of the word "God" constantly changes, so that it would seem better to introduce new terms for new concepts. There is an enormous difference between a personal deity who knows and cares what I am up to and an abstract intelligence permeating or constituting the universe. Using the same word for these two extreme concepts can lead to confusion.

When the theory of evolution, along with those of the rest of rapidly developing science, made its enormous impact in the mid-1800s, the leaders of Western religion had a limited number of options.

One approach is to reject those aspects of science that disagree with doctrine as bad science on the grounds that whatever is inconsistent with revealed truth must be wrong. This effort was supported by a number of devout scientists who then looked for errors in Darwin's facts and theories as a source of refutation. It is still the viewpoint of those scientifically oriented fundamentalists who periodically persuade legislators to insist that "creation science" be taught in public schools.

A second approach is to assert that religion is a matter of faith whose mysteries are totally other than those of the world of science. This allows or forces adherents to divide their lives into noncommunicating compartments, accepting the "truths" of each as valid within its own domain.

Another option is to embrace both scripture and evolution; reinterpreting the Bible so as to be in accord with the findings of science. Although rejecting the absolute truth of Genesis, many accept the absolute validity of later books of the Bible. An extreme version of this approach is to give up Scripture as a source of knowledge and accept it as a source of inspiration. This leads to a deism embedded in Western historical tradition.

All paths are taken by twentieth-century religious groups, but none with the exception of the most intellectually isolated and introverted sects escape from some reaction to the apple of knowledge nibbled on by Darwin and his colleagues. While nineteenth-century religious thought was thrown in temporary disarray by the advances in biology and geology, science also underwent changes as a result of the bitter struggles being waged. In response to the conflict, many scientists sought a position that would free them from the battle against accepted religious doctrine and leave them to deal with the wealth of confusing data that was accumulating. Thomas Huxley coined the word "agnostic" to express his uncommitted position. Biologists tended to the view that nothing could be concluded about religious belief from the results of their studies. With the advent of genetics and knowledge of the random nature of mutations, that position hardened. Many researchers decided that questions of meaning were entirely outside their scope.

That tendency to divorce the content of biology from

any metaphysical issues has been a major theme for over a century. It is restated in the idiom of molecular biology by Jacques Monod, whose views are certainly representative of a large number of contemporary biologists. In the book *Chance and Necessity* (1971) he states, "The basic premise of the scientific method [is] . . . that nature is *objective* not *projective*." By objective he means that the laws of nature have no purpose other than their existence. He elaborates: "We can not attribute any design, any project or purpose to nature." The rigor with which he adheres to this is evidenced: "But the postulate of objectivity is consubstantial with science: it has guided the whole of its prodigious development for three centuries. There is no way to be rid of it."

In terms of our prior discussion, Monod's insistence on nature's objectivity as a basic methodological principle of science seems unnecessary. In Margenau's scheme, such a statement would constitute a new metaphysical criterion; given the choice, we choose *objective* constructs over *projective* constructs. Such a metaphysical criterion is not introduced because in many cases we have no way of preknowing if a construct is projective or not. Only after developing a mature, coherent science can we ask about purpose or meaning. Huxley's search for freedom led to Monod's putting a heavy metaphysical yoke on science as he tried to bar that discipline from helping us understand vital aspects of our existence.

In short, the postulate of objectivity is a good political ploy for scientists to put distance between themselves and theologians, but there is no valid philosophical reason why it must enter science as a basic premise. We can formulate our natural philosophy with no commitment one way or the other about nature's objectivity and then later raise questions about meaning.

Monod goes further than the methodological denial of purpose. He labels any attempt to find meaning in the scientific study of the universe as "animism." This deliberate denigration of the search for purpose by the blatant choice of a pejorative word indicates the depth of his disdain for those who disagree with his philosophy. He thus aims his heavy artillery at Pierre Teilhard de Chardin in a mean-spirited and vicious attack on Teilhard's evolutionary approach.

In his final attempt to convince one of the purposelessness of the universe, Monod argues that everything we see in the living world is the result of chance and that it is not possible to predict the existence of the life from the laws of physics. Since far-from-equilibrium thermodynamics, the theory of dissipative structures, synergetics, and other theories of self-organizing systems were incompletely formulated when Monod wrote his monograph (and are still incompletely formulated), he was asserting what yet undeveloped branches of physics would be unable to do. Indeed, he was so eager to make everything the result of chance that he abandoned the scientist's usual caution of withholding from predicting what future science will or will not be able to accomplish. In short, the author of *Chance and Necessity* was so determined to eradicate purpose that he transmogrified his versions of both science and philosophy.

What started out as Thomas Huxley's attempt to free science from religion ended one hundred years later with Jacques Monod's assertion: "The biosphere is a unique occurrence non reducible from first principles." That is exactly what certain theologians would assert, after which they would continue defining it as a sacred mystery to be seen only through the eye of faith. Once an event is unique in the Monod sense, all explanations are equally plausible; the event is effectively removed from the methodology of science and must be considered as history.

The total randomness advocated by Monod represents one of the extremes to emerge from this "hundred-year war," but an equally forceful theory on another side was published in 1975. *The Troubled Waters of Evolution* is the updated, resurrected account of fundamentalism written by Henry M. Morris. It represents the view of the Creation Research Society. "To be a voting member, one must have either a Master's Degree or a Ph.D. in one of the natural sciences and must also subscribe to a Statement of Faith which includes commitment to belief in special creation and a worldwide Noahic flood, as well as opposition to any form of evolution—including theistic evolution." Note that while all philosophies of science agree that there is a tentative character to knowledge that can be changed by experimental evidence, this "Research Society" requires a commitment to unchanging knowledge in advance of examining any experimental evidence and in disregard of future developments.

The fundamentalist scientists use the language of science if not the spirit to phrase their arguments. They are experts at assessing weaknesses in our understanding of mechanisms of evolution, and by everybody's standards there are many weaknesses. They invoke the second law of thermodynamics and the tendency to disorder to argue against evolution, yet, like Monod, they seem to ignore the wealth of modern material on self-organization in systems undergoing energy flows. (We'll want to get to those thoughts later.) Morris categorically states: "Order never spontaneously arises out of disorder." This statement is in total disagreement with experience. Just look out the window at those lovely shapely, fleecy clouds that have condensed out of totally disordered gas-phase water molecules.

After 190 pages, Morris gets to his real point: "We must conclude, therefore, that if the Bible is really the Word of God (as its writers allege and as we believe) then evolution and its geological age-system must be completely false." He has previously hinted, "then Satan himself is the originator of the concept of evolution."

Morris is also explicit in stating what future science will not do. "The study of biochemistry and terrestrial environments can never explain the origin of life." This comes close to Monod's assertion that "the biosphere is a unique occurrence non reducible from first principles." The archopponents have curiously come to the same conclusion, one because he is certain he knows the answers and the second because he is certain they are unknowable.

Jacques Monod and Henry M. Morris are important as representatives of what the public envisions as the scientific and religious points of polarization. Accepting one is to build in unnecessary metaphysical criteria that remove science from the search for meaning. To accept the other is to deny the epistemological foundations upon which science is built and to replace them with a statement of faith prior to the science. If that's the best we can do, I want to go back to the oily bilge for some more thinking.

CHAPTER 5

Rocks of Ages

Today the example set by my role models has been violated. I lack their discipline to stay in one place. The excuse—the less indulgent would call it a rationalization—is that I want to think about the lithosphere, and this activity will be enhanced by getting in touch with the material of that domain. So on this particular Sunday morning I find myself at Ulupalakua hiking along the western slopes of Mount Haleakala, the House of the Sun.

Since all four geospheres are highly interactive and life is a property of all features of the planet, any geosphere could have been chosen to begin my story. The lithosphere has been picked because it is the oldest and largest of the four and because some members of the hiking club have asked me to join them. In addition, it's much on my mind, because plate tectonics provides a good deal of the impetus for this year's work.

At an elevation a few thousand feet above the sea, one can look down at the deep blue of La Pérouse Bay. The lava from the most recent flow two hundred years ago has left blackened stains on the countryside that are still visible. In the dryness of southwest Maui the basalt weathers very slowly. Beneath our feet an older lava has crumbled and turned red from oxidation and the acids produced by living organisms. While examining the black lava more carefully, one notices that the occasional plants and microorganisms growing on it provide information about the ecological succession that will one day convert this hardened rock to soil.

Turning south, I see the outline of the big island of Hawaii rising dramatically out of the sea. Mauna Kea and Mauna Loa are clearly visible, pointing thousands of feet into the atmosphere. Unseen behind these main peaks is Kilauea, where, according to local legend, Pele, the Fire Goddess, has found her home. Madame Pele, according to the kahuna priests, periodically bursts forth in anger or sheer playfulness spilling molten lava from the peaks or flanks of the mountains. Geologists attribute this to the buildup of basaltic crust due to the extrusion of molten magma. Whichever language one uses, a volcanic eruption is an awesome event that induces fear and trembling. Many years ago I stood beside a caldera on the slopes of Kilauea and looked into a sea of molten lava. The world has seemed less permanent since that time.

North along the trail is an old, tiny white Congregational church maintained in good condition but rarely used. These islands are dotted with churches, for the parish sizes were limited by walking distance to the sanctuaries. Nonetheless, the number of congregations is also a measure of the vigor of the missionaries in seeking converts. The overt hedonism of present-day Hawaii as compared with the missionary era may in part be related to the public impact of those events that followed the voyage of the *Beagle*.

On the trail, with feet cinder-deep in the lithosphere, one has time to contemplate what we know about the hard stuff of our planet. It is trite but true to say that a quiet revolution has taken place in geological thought in the past generation. This shift in our picture of continents and mountains is as radical a step for geology as the Copernican shift to a moving earth was for astronomy. The earth, which at the continental level had been seen as rigid and unchanging, is now viewed as excitingly dynamic and in constant motion. Progress in geophysics is so rapid that any statement we make today may be subject to revision tomorrow or next week. All views must be approached with some tolerance.

To put the lithosphere in place, one had best start at the core of the structure, which in this case is the hot iron- and nickel-rich metallic center of the planet. This inner sphere is two thousand miles in radius and is embedded in the center of the globe like a large pit in a round fruit; the avocado comes to mind. This part of the planet also has a structure that need not concern us at the moment. We should know, however, that some sort of geodynamic flow of molten ferrous metal in the iron-rich core is responsible for the earth's magnetic field. The core is surrounded by a seventeen-hundred-mile-thick shell called the mantle, a layer of silicate minerals, rock, and melted rock. Surrounding the mantle is another, much thinner, shell of varying thickness, which is the actual crust. There are two kinds of crust—the thicker, less dense, continental variety and the thinner, denser, oceanic type. On top of this outer layer sit most of the hydrosphere, biosphere, and atmosphere.

The crust and outer sixty or so miles of the mantle constitute the lithosphere of modern-day geophysics. Just below the lithosphere, going down a few hundred miles, we find the asthenosphere (a most unaesthetic word). This layer is sufficiently hot that over a long-enough time scale it very slowly flows, allowing the lithosphere to slide along.

The fundamental principle of modern geological theory is that the whole of the lithosphere is made up of a small number of large plates that are moving around with respect to each other. As a result, the surface of the earth is in a dynamic state, with continents drifting hither and yon. This thought has shaken the foundations of contemporary geophysics and presented us with a new vision of our old planet. The stable world of the nineteenth-century theologians is gone, and the ground beneath our feet becomes part of a vast cycle of change.

The idea of moving continents is so strange to me that I have to keep restating it. There is a fascinating collection of articles in *Scientific American* entitled "Continents Adrift" and "Continents Aground." Those articles describe the surface of our globe as made up of an irregular mosaic of rigid plates. These plates, the largest of which underlies almost the entire Pacific Ocean, are about one hundred miles deep and sit on a fluid layer of partially melted rock. Plates move apart, come together, or slide past each other: each of these types of motions produces planetary activity seen in earthquakes, volcanoes, and mountain uplifting.

The theory of drifting continents was proposed and vigorously defended during the first third of the twentieth century by German meteorologist Alfred Wegener. He argued that the extraordinarily good fit of the shapes of the land areas on the two sides of the Atlantic meant that they were once part of a gigantic continent that had drifted apart.

Geologists did not accept continental drift until the 1960s, when new evidence came from studies of the magnetism of the Atlantic sea floor and other subterranean surfaces. Much data has accumulated showing that the earth's magnetic field, the same field that directs the compass on my boat, changes direction every thirty thousand years or so. When fresh lava hardens, it has a slight magnetic polarity due to being oriented in the earth's field. By towing a recording magnetometer behind a boat, it is possible to obtain detailed information about the magnetism of the ocean floor as a function of position.

Such measurements convinced scientists that the ocean floor is formed by undersea volcanic activity at midocean ridges. The bottom then spreads out at right angles to the ridge. Thus the volcanic activity at the Mid-Atlantic Ridge is separating the Americas from Europe and Africa An overwhelming amount of geomagnetic evidence has now accumulated, and almost all geologists are convinced that plate tectonics and continental drift provide an explanatory theory for most of the large-scale geological structure of the earth's surface. Geology has undergone a paradigm shift, and we face the consequences of the new viewpoint.

A general axiom of physics states that dynamic processes must be energy-driven, and plate tectonics is no exception. Within the core and mantle of the earth are substantial quantities of radioactive materials, principally thorium, uranium, and potassium 40. The energy of their radioactive decay, added to that of gravitational condensation, is converted to heat, making the interior of the planet hotter than the surface. Since heat flows from hot to cold, there is an outward transport through the core and mantle to the crust.

Heat flow, as my general-science teacher drummed into our heads many years ago, occurs by three processes; conduction, convection, and radiation. Convection involves less dense, hot material rising against gravity and colder, denser material correspondingly sinking. Such action is occurring somewhere in the mantle. Even though the materials are barely fluid, some 25 million cubic miles convectively rises each year from the mantle to the lithosphere, and correspondingly 25 million cubic miles of colder rock is cycled back into the interior. The heat energy arriving at the surface is transferred to the atmosphere, where it is radiated to outer space.

We are being treated to a splendid and grandiose example of thermodynamics that must later be considered in more detail. The physical law states that *the flow of energy through a system acts to organize that system.* I first wrote those words in 1968. They were quoted in the *Whole Earth Catalog* and became a kind of bridge between poetry, physics, and ecology. I'm happy about that. Energy in this case is flowing from a source (it is stored as mass energy in radioactive nuclei and as gravitational potential) to a sink (the cold of outer space). The flow of that energy through the intermediate system (the lithosphere) is organizing the system into plates, continents, mountains, and many of the other interesting features that I see around me and feel under my feet. This all too, too solid earth exhibits much more action than we suspected. It's a matter of looking at the right time scale.

The processes taking place at the intersection of plates are *spreading, subduction,* and *sliding.* The most thoroughly studied is the separation of plates accompanied by sea floor spreading. The best-characterized line of spreading, mentioned above, is the Mid-Atlantic Ridge, which runs from Iceland to the latitude of Southern Patagonia and is responsible for the Americas having separated from Europe and Africa. Some hundreds of millions of years ago most of the land area of the world was part of one supercontinent. A ridge developed, splitting off the American plate, which has continually drifted westward. These drifts are quite slow on a human time scale, less than one inch per year, but on a geological time scale this involves considerable motion. For example, that inch per year is twelve miles every million years. At that rate a disturbance could move halfway around the world in a billion years.

Along the Mid-Atlantic Ridge, magma (subcrustal molten material) within the mantle rises up, pushing back the plates on either side, creating new sea floor. This new material beneath the ocean acts on the new world plate, separating it progressively farther from the old. Since sea floor is constantly being created while the total ocean area remains about constant, the floor must somewhere be disappearing into the mantle. Confirmation of this disappearance was already available in the evidence, based on the study of sedimentary fossils, that no part of the ocean floor is more than 200 million years old in spite of the fact that the earth is 4.5 billion years in age.

The explanation is simple and dramatic. Where two plates approach, one slides over the other and the lower one is pushed down (subducted) into the mantle and becomes part of it. Just as material rises out of the subsurface, rock is forced back into that zone in a cyclic process characteristic of all long-term dynamic systems.

West of South America from Colombia to Argentina is the Nazca plate, bounded on the west by the East Pacific Ridge. The sea floor spreading from the ridge pushes this plate eastward, where it abuts the large South American plate, which is being forced westward by the activities of the Mid-Atlantic Ridge. The South American plate moves up on top of the Nazca plate, forcing the latter down into the mantle. The western edge of South America is uplifted by the subduction process, giving rise to the Andes mountain range. Thus the *alta plana*, the high plains, at thirteen thousand feet are rich in fossils of marine mollusks, a reminder of the period before the rise when that part of the crust was continental shelf. I recall once wandering through the streets of La Paz, Bolivia, where street urchins sell both shards of Inca pottery and fossils of shells laid down when this area was sea floor. For a few pennies one can obtain authentic relics of the archeological and pale-ontological past of that great city.

The Indian plate (sometimes called the Australian plate) runs from Pakistan to New Zealand in a north-west to southeast arc, and extends south to the Antarctic plate. The Mid-Indian Ridge is a source of sea floor spreading that drives the Indian plate northward and somewhat eastward. Where it abuts the Eurasian plate, over a fourteen-hundred-mile line, the Indian plate sub-ducts under the Eurasian, giving rise to the Himalayas, the world's highest mountains. To the east, where the Indian subducts under the Pacific plate, it gives rise to the Solomon–New Hebrides Islands arc. In all cases the underriding material sinks down into the mantle, be-comes melted, and is recycled into the stuff out of which new lithosphere is made.

At the west coast of North America the Pacific plate is moving northward relative to the North American plate in a sliding motion that involves no spreading or subduction. The line of demarcation is the San Andreas fault system, which is subject to great seismic activity that periodically relieves the compression built up by the two-inch-a-year northern slide of the large oceanic plate.

The great San Francisco earthquake of 1906 is an example of this activity. More major seismic tremors are anticipated in this part of the world.

The lithosphere on which I'm hiking at Ulupalakua has apparently been produced by an eruption through a plate moving over an underlying hot spot going down into the earth's interior. This same process can be seen at hundreds of sites around the world. Such formations involve magma coming up out of the earth, amassing on top of the plate, and hardening into the solid material that cools while warming the hearts of realtors.

Because I am surrounded by lava and materials that have been derived from lava, there is insufficient attention being paid to the other ways that solid portions of the surface of the earth can form. When magma rises from the interior and cools under pressure below the surface, igneous rocks, such as granite, result. Volcanic mountains are formed by magma breaking through and pouring forth as basalt. Other mountains are formed by uplift, the magma pushing up from below and hardening. Depending on detailed conditions during cooling and the exact chemical composition, thousands of different kinds of minerals can form. The variety and beauty of some of these minerals can be seen in museum and other rock collections.

Even stone is not permanent. Wind, rain, the roots of plants, and the organic acids secreted by living things eat away at rocks, dissolve chemicals, and crack boulders, eventually wearing them down to sand and pebbles. These small pieces can collect into sediments, which may become buried and subjected to higher pressures and temperatures. The small particles are recompacted into sedimentary rocks like shales and all of the fossil-containing deposits that include remains of living organisms along with the rock debris. We are thus left with nature's record of former ages. This record troubled nineteenth-century religious thinkers and still animates the discussion of evolution. The importance of these sedimentary deposits in the arguments between science and religion lends whimsical symbolic significance to the most significant legal battle in the last fifty years of this dispute taking place in Little Rock.

Broken rocks may undergo another fate. In areas of high enough rainfall, the small pieces of cooled magma combine with roots and decaying organic material, as well as bacteria, insects, worms, and all manner of subterranean creatures to give rise to soil. On the island of Hawaii there are areas where new lava flows exist that are originally sterile, devoid of all life because of the searing heat of the molten lava. In ten years one can return and see algae and lichens growing in the wet cracks that formed when the lava cooled. In twenty years tiny ferns come up from the crevices, the surface begins to break up, and the zones of growth spread out from the crevice. And so it goes. In areas where the flow has taken place four hundred years ago, there are now metrosideros forests, and the hard black lava has become the red soil characteristic of volcanic islands. Soil is neither biosphere nor lithosphere but a dynamic combination of the two, an interdependent system. This interdependence is true everywhere, but is easiest to see in the postvolcanic succession where an entire forest evolves from a lifeless lava flow.

The new geology not only speaks of the massive movements of continents and tectonic plates, but also reminds us that the entire globe undergoes convective flows that constantly freshen the earth with new lithosphere and recycle old, tired sediments. The earth's mantle has been described as a shell of silicate that lies above the metallic core and is warmed by the decay of radioactive isotopes. Within the uppermost four hundred miles, the heat drives massive convective currents, pushing up mantle material into the crust while capturing sinking slabs of material from the crust. Consideration of the long-time scale makes it difficult to comprehend just how dynamic a planet we live on, but that is precisely the message of contemporary science. Just as the great ecological cycles keep regenerating the biological materials of our planet, so the great convective cycles of the mantle keep regenerating the lithosphere. Both sets of cycles are intimately connected with the habitability of our planet.

As I step one foot in front of the other on the seemingly solid ground beneath my feet, I recapture from memory some lines of Walt Whitman about recycling in the biosphere:

Now I am terrified at the Earth! it is that calm and patient,
It grows such sweet things out of such corruptions,
It turns harmless and stainless on its axis, with such endless
*   successions of diseas'd corpses,*
It distills such exquisite winds out of such infused fetor,

It renews with such unwitting looks, its prodigal, annual,
    sumptuous crops,
It gives such divine materials to men, and accepts such leav-
    ings from them at last.

I'm going to leave off thinking about the lithosphere
for a little while; one must spend some time contemplating the processes of plate tectonics and mantle dynamics.
Because the movements are massive and the rates relatively slow, we must attune our minds to a whole new
mode of thought.

The hike is on its final lap, and we're descending the
slope back toward the road. The path to the car passes a
local winery, and we cannot resist stopping for a sample
of pineapple wine. A sip leads to the purchase of a
bottle, shared with my hiking companions. That
definitely slows down any thoughts of geophysical
processes, and I return to the boat. Sitting in the cockpit, we watch the sun set over the hydrosphere above
the Pacific plate. Slowly the stars come out. In time both
the North Star and Southern Cross are visible, Polaris
and Crux assuring us of where we are in the universe.

CHAPTER 6

Energy Flow

I'm not going to be writing on the boat today. In fact, I'm standing on the gasoline dock watching the movable desk sailing off to Honolulu. Once every year or two it is taken to dry dock, pulled out of the water, cleaned, and painted; at least those portions below the waterline are so treated. The reason for this troublesome and expensive procedure is that algae, barnacles, and all manner of flora and fauna grow on the underwater surface and will, if allowed to continue, convert the boat into a reef or island that will eventually become stationary in one way or another.

To prevent this bottom growth, the surface is painted with the most toxic, long-lasting preparation that the chemical industry can produce within the limits of the law. After all, it would be foolish for painters to become seriously ill just to protect the boats. There is a constant war being waged between the research divisions of chemical manufacturers and marine organisms. The failure of the technologists to utterly devastate the biota is a good sign for those who worry about our planet's being poisoned until life can no longer be sustained. If the most concerted efforts of chemists to do in oceanic surface dwellers have failed, it seems most unlikely that our random mistakes will totally overcome the resiliency of life. We may foul things up from the point of view of aesthetics or human habitation, but our chance of making the entire planet uninhabitable for all eco-systems is virtually negligible. That may not come as overwhelming good news to those who are concerned with nuclear disarmament and other pressing issues, but I am personally comforted by the thought of the continued biotic activity on Mother Earth.

As the sails go up and the boat moves off, I transfer my operation to the Lahaina Library. That institution is not yet open, reminding me that I've spent a fair amount of my life standing in front of libraries waiting for them to open. It always recalls Omar's words:

> While the cock crowed
> Those who stood before the tavern
> Shouted, Open then the door
> For the bird of time has little way to flutter
> And once departed may return no more.

I once recited this poem at the door of a science library at Yale when it opened a few minutes late, but alas, the thoughts were somehow lost on the librarian.

While not one of the world's research centers, the

Lahaina Public Library contains some old friends, like the *Handbook of Chemistry and Physics* and the *Encyclopedia of Philosophy*. Seated at the tables are new friends, like the young man who has dropped out of an MBA program at McGill University and now reads poetry all day, or the lady who is catching up with the latest magazines while waiting for a sailboat to take her down to the isolation of the Line Islands. I'm psychologically ready, however, to forgo conversation and get back to unifying thoughts about earth, air, fire, and water.

Now that we have looked at some issues of science and religion, it is time to set down a preliminary coherent scientific overview of the world in which we live. If this is done with a minimum of philosophical precon-

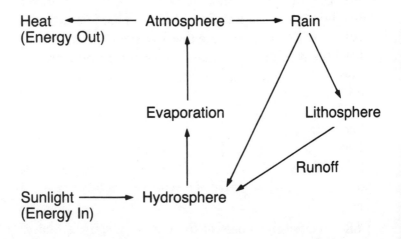

THE HYDROLOGICAL CYCLE

ditions, we can first assimilate the accumulated information and then later begin to think about what it means.

Having adopted the geochemists' categories, the next step is to summarize what is happening in each of the four domains. After looking at the lithosphere from an initial perspective, one suspects that the most interesting features of the globe may be involved in what's taking place in the flows of matter and energy between the geospheres. We start by examining the water exchanges.

The oceans, rivers, and lakes of the world continually receive energy from the sun, which heats the surface waters, causing them to evaporate and move into the atmosphere as vapor. As the water molecules rise into the upper layers, they give off heat, some of which radiates into outer space. The water molecules thus cool and condense into clouds of liquid droplets. These clouds in time become unstable and fall as rain or snow. The water reaching the land eventually runs off and finds its way back to rivers and ultimately to the sea. We are describing two flows that go in cycles: water to air and back again to water, and water to air to groundwater to rivers and oceans. The example exhibits two principles about continuous exchange among the geospheres. First, the flows must occur in cycles or else one or more of the compartments will empty out. For example, if the flow of water to air and then to land did not complete the loop by runoff, all the water would end up on the soggy ground and the process would come to a halt. The second, less obvious, principle is that these cyclic flows of matter are driven by energy moving through the system. In the water cycle just discussed, the energy comes from sunlight and leaves as radiant heat given off by the atmosphere to outer space. Matter cycles and energy flows. That simple statement is necessary to understand our world. It can also be demonstrated for the well-known ecological carbon cycle.

In the process of photosynthesis, which is driven by sunlight, carbon dioxide moves from the atmosphere into plant materials. The plants are either eaten by animals or decay, and carbon dioxide is returned to the atmosphere by metabolism, which is slow combustion. These biological activities give off heat that eventually becomes part of the energy radiated by the planet into outer space. Once again, matter is moving around a cycle and energy is flowing through the system.

We can combine all the basic flows that take place between the geospheres.

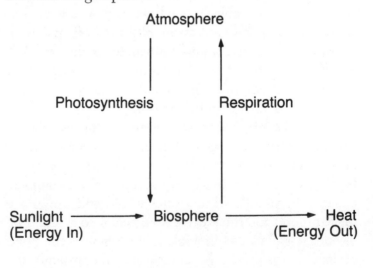

THE CARBON CYCLE

84

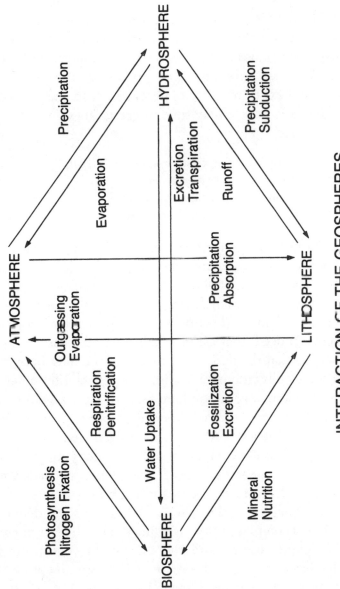

INTERACTION OF THE GEOSPHERES

The drawing represents the strong interrelatedness of all processes occurring on our planet, and the whole diagram can also be broken down into simpler cycles of the kind we have just been discussing. No event or structure exists in isolation. Our attempt to grasp all the relations at the same time suggests these words of Alexander Pope:

> *Who sees with equal eye, as God of all,*
> *A hero perish or a sparrow fall,*
> *Atoms or systems into ruin hurl'd,*
> *And now a bubble burst, and now a world.*

In scientific language, one can say that the great geospheres of the world are constantly exchanging material with each other and that these exchanges lead to a mutual rejuvenation. Living organisms are particularly active in giving and taking material from other compartments. Indeed, that activity leads us to the basis of our theme—that the dynamic activities of the biosphere are so completely interrelated with those of the lithosphere, hydrosphere, and atmosphere that we must regard continuous life on earth as a general property of the entire planet and its star rather than as a restricted feature of individual, isolated organisms. The underlying idea for this totally integrative view of the planet was stated in 1979 by J. E. Lovelock in the book *Gaia* (Greek for "Earth Goddess"). He wrote: "We have since defined Gaia as a complex entity involving the Earth's biosphere, atmosphere, oceans and soil; the totality constituting a feedback or cybernetic system which seeks an optimum physical and chemical environment for life on this planet." I don't follow all the implications of Lovelock's assumptions about self-regulating properties, but I recognize the importance of his contribution in stressing the unity of planetary life. Some of these ideas were also suggested sixty-three years earlier, in Lawrence J. Henderson's book *The Fitness of the Environment*.

These are pretty heady thoughts for the Lahaina Public Library, but that is the nice thing about a completely connected view of the world. Wherever you happen to be standing, you are in the middle of the action.

The pictures we have been drawing with boxes and arrows place our discussion in the field of systems theory, a formal discipline that tries to understand integrated activities of the whole in terms of the properties and interactions of the parts.

One ever-present but sometimes unseen feature on our diagrams is the previously mentioned flow of energy that powers all the dynamic processes and results in the cycling of matter. Aside from buying gas for the Atomic 4 and jogging in the morning, I haven't been focusing much on energy lately, but the time has clearly come to bear down on that all-important construct and see how it fits into the story. During a previous fallow time in Hawaii many years ago, I had written a monograph, *Energy Flow in Biology*, so this is sort of a nostalgic return to that subject. The reasons for focusing on energy are, however, not confined to nostalgia; the energy concept is central to an understanding of earth, air, fire, and water. Indeed, it is central to all of physics, chemistry, and biology.

"Energy" has become one of the most used, overused, and misused words of our time, yet in each of its contexts no synonym quite seems adequate to convey the same vigor and thrust. Since the mid-1800s energy has been the single most important idea in physics, and the understanding and measurement of that quantity has been developed with increasing precision. In spite of all the present-day talk of energy, the subject involves subtle ideas that must be grasped gingerly. I like to raise the question "How would I explain energy to my neighbors on nearby boats if they were willing to listen to me?" I haven't had the courage to try this on either Doug or John, but the spiel would go something like this:

Energy is an abstract concept; you can't see it or feel it, even if you have to pay for it. There's no way to seriously think about energy without being willing to get into abstractions. Of course, love and joy and sorrow are also abstract concepts. We can usually understand them without much problem, although dealing with them may be an entirely different matter.

Force is a related but easier idea than energy, because we can reduce it to the everyday experience of a pull or a push. The modern age of mechanics began when Isaac Newton in 1690 took the idea of force from daily life and put it into formal mathematical language by stating that the strength of a force can be measured by how rapidly it accelerates a material object. An elaborate technology developed for the measurement of these quantities. Suppose I apply a force to a physical object, as in pulling on a child's wagon. There are three things

88

that might happen, either separately or together: the wagon might be accelerated, the wagon might be pulled uphill against gravity, the bearings and tires might heat up from friction.

The quantity calculated by multiplying the force times the distance over which it is exerted is defined as the *work* that is done on the wagon. This is related to the sweat-of-the-brow kind of work, but it is a formal mathematical way of assigning a number to the concept. A description of my walking up a hill pulling a wagon behind me includes the fact that I am doing work and it is being converted into motion, gravitational potential, and heat. This interconversion means that work, motion, gravitational potential, and heat must all have something in common. What they share is that they are all forms of energy. That conclusion is not obvious but was developed with great intellectual effort in the period 1840–50. The first major breakthrough in that study was formulating the law of conservation of energy, which stated that for a closed system (no flows in or out) the amount of energy is constant: it can be transformed from one form to another, but it can't be created or destroyed.

Interestingly enough, in this port setting I am reminded that the law of conservation of energy, like the theory of evolution, was the result of a long sea voyage. On February 22, 1840, Julius Robert von Mayer, who has been called the prophet of energy, embarked from Rotterdam as ship's doctor on the sailing vessel *Java* headed for Indonesia. The subsequent events have been reported by a biographer of Mayer's, Robert Bruce Lindsay.

The voyage took three months . . . the ship's doctor did not have much work to do, had little association with the ship's officers . . . and spent a large fraction of his time reading scientific books he had brought with him. There seems, however, to have been nothing in this reading to prepare him for the discovery he made shortly after arrival in the roadstead of Surabaya in East Java, when he had occasion to let blood from some of the sailors on the ship. He was surprised to find the venous blood a much brighter red than expected, and at first thought he had struck an artery. Discussion with physicians in the East Indies, however, verified that this was a common observation in the Tropics. This observation, taking place around the middle of July 1840, was the spark that set off the whole train of Mayer's thought culminating in the generalization of the concept of energy. The redness of the venous blood means less oxidation of the food consumed and hence less heat produced. The person living in the Tropics does not need this heat and hence will not oxidize as much food material. This stimulated a train of thought in Mayer, in which the work done by bodily exertion also entered. . . . Once Mayer had become excited with this biophysical puzzle he was obsessed by it and its scientific consequences for the rest of his professional career.

The doctor returned to Europe and began work on his classic "On the Quantitative and Qualitative Determination of Forms of Energy." That paper is recognized as the first general statement of the law of conservation of energy.

At this stage in my telling John or Doug about energy, they would begin to get fidgety and I'd have to offer them a beer to get them to keep listening. Since I can't offer readers a beer, I have to offer a reminder that knowledge of energy is vitally important and it's hard to think seriously about any scientific subject except butterfly collecting without understanding the basic facts about energy. Even the serious study of butterflies requires a consideration of energy budgets.

The conservation principle can be shown by an example such as a weight suspended by a rope hanging from the boom of my boat. If I keep the rope taut and lift the weight, I am doing work against gravity, and therefore, the weight has gravitational energy. If I release the weight, it swings back and forth like a pendulum. At the bottom of the swing there is no gravitational energy beyond what the weight initially possessed, but the speed is at its maximum. The energy is thus all kinetic (energy of motion). At the top of the swing, motion momentarily stops; there is no kinetic energy, but gravitational energy is greatest. Energy keeps changing between the two forms, but at each cycle the weight does not swing quite so high. Friction with the air and at the boom are generating heat, so that less gravitational energy is available. Eventually the weight stops swinging, and all the energy is heat.

A second example consists of an electric battery, a motor, a series of pulleys, a weight, and a generator. At first, the energy is all chemical potential stored in the battery, which can be used to drive the motor and lift the weight. A portion of the energy is now in gravitational potential. The weight can be hooked up so that when it falls it turns the generator, converting the energy of motion into electrical energy, which may be used to charge the battery. This cycle can be continuously repeated, but at each stage some energy is converted to heat until finally the battery becomes completely discharged and the original chemical potential is now entirely lost.

These examples demonstrate another property of energy—its tendency to end up as heat. It is relatively easy to transform various forms of energy into each other, but difficult to change heat back into other types with high efficiency. Of course, the possibility of transformation exists, as witnessed by heat engines, but no one has been able to build an engine that converts more than a certain fraction of the heat energy of a system into gravitational potential or some other form. Physicists can calculate that fraction using a mathematical formula first developed more than one hundred and fifty years ago. There is something special about heat because it is energy associated with the motion of atoms and molecules at the submicroscopic level. The fraction of this energy that is not available to do work is measured by another precise and abstract quantity, the entropy. We now understand that entropy, which was originally introduced to deal with the efficiency of engines, is a very special quantity that measures the disorder of material at the atomic and molecular level.

The tendency of energy to become randomly distributed in the kinetic form among molecules is the basis of the famous second law of thermodynamics. There are almost as many statements of this law as there are thermodynamicists, but all of them convey the idea that in an isolated system entropy will increase. Thus heat flows from a hotter to a colder body, and molecules diffuse from a higher to a lower concentration. A system moving toward equilibruim assumes the most disordered molecular state consistent with the conditions under which it is maintained. At equilibrium everything is completely homogeneous and nothing interesting can happen.

At this point I would offer Doug or John another beer and go on. Traditional thermodynamics is based on two great generalizations, the conservation of energy (the first law) and the increase of entropy (the second law). Using these principles, it is possible to learn a great deal about equilibrium systems. They are either immersed in a constant-temperature heat bath (isothermal system) or isolated by placing them in containers that are insulated and therefore allow no heat flow (adiabatic isolation). Given a limited amount of information about these kinds of systems, thermodynamics makes it possible to calculate (predict) additional information about quantities such as pressure, temperature, density, concentration, surface tension, and electrode potentials.

Curiously enough, the laws of thermodynamics we have been discussing were formulated at about the same time as the theory of evolution was being stated and debated. This led to an apparent contradiction between physics and biology, and reverberations of that argument are still heard today. The laws of inanimate matter indicate that the world is moving toward a state of maximum disorder, while the history of life shows a progression from simplicity to higher and higher forms of complexity leading up to *Homo sapiens*, a physically improbable group of objects. Evolution speaks of progress and advancement, while the second law foretells of decay into disorder and the heat death of the universe.

The discrepancy was faced and resolved by physicist Ludwig Boltzmann over a hundred years ago. Strangely, his solution has gone unheeded by many, so that some contemporary writers still put forth wondrous and imaginative ideas about entropy and evolution. Evangelists, evolutionists, environmentalists, and economists often misunderstand the thermodynamic problem and draw strange conclusions about life and the second law. The answer is much simpler than most futurists and entropic pessimists assume and much less miraculous than the fundamentalists are willing to accept.

The second law of thermodynamics states that energetically isolated systems and systems surrounded by a uniform heat bath (isothermal) tend toward a maximum of molecular disorder. There seems to be no reason to question the law. All relevant experimental evidence makes it as valid today as when first formulated in the mid-1800s. The catch is that, except in the laboratory, we almost never deal with isolated or isothermal systems, so that the law is a limiting approximation for certain quite restricted situations. The approach of thermodynamics provides deep insights, but we must always be careful to apply it to situations for which its validity has been established.

What we experience in the everyday world are not equilibrium situations but objects that are sites of energy flows from sources of that wondrous stuff to sinks. A sink is a low-temperature object with a one-way flow of energy; it enters but does not leave. For flow systems a new qualitative rule emerges, which has been called the fourth law of thermodynamics and states that intermediate systems undergoing flows of energy from sources to sinks organize themselves. The flow of energy orders the system through which it flows. Although the fourth law lacks the mathematical precision with which the others may be stated, it is nonetheless just as valid and as firmly rooted in the physical laws underlying both biology and the earth sciences. We are unable to predict precisely what organization will take place on a planet, for that depends on molecular details, but we can be assured that under energy flow the planetary surfaces or any other systems will inexorably evolve to more organized states. The fourth law is a new insight for our time, and it renders natural all of the order that we see around us.

This new rule of thermodynamics in no way violates the second law. (If there is some worry that we are ignoring the third law, that relationship deals with another issue, the entropy of pure substances at the absolute zero of temperature, and is not central to the present discussion.) If we include the sources and sinks of energy, then all the parts taken together constitute an isolated system and the total entropy of the whole increases. There can thus be a regional ordering, a local decrease of entropy at the expense of an entropy increase of the source and the sink. Indeed, since the known universe contains energy sources such as stars, and the giant sink of interstellar and intergalactic space, other objects such as planetary surfaces will be subject to constant ordering influences and will be maintained away from that equilibrium condition where entropy is maximized.

Planet Earth has three major energy sources and one principal sink. The greatest flow is from the sun, which daily bathes us in a stream of electromagnetic radiation and drives the processes of the atmosphere, hydrosphere, and biosphere and also contributes to those of the lithosphere. The second major source of energy is the heat generated by decay of radioactive nuclei in the interior of the planet. This source provides power for much of the dynamics of the solid portions of the planet, lithospheric cycling and tectonic movement. The third input comes from the mechanics of the solar system and the gravitation interaction of the heavenly bodies. I daily experience the effect of this process by stepping into the boat from the dock at different levels, because the tide regularly raises and lowers the vessels in the harbor. The hydrosphere is most affected, but the other domains also feel the tug of the sun and the moon and the effects of such gravitational pulls.

The sink for energy from the earth is the cold blackness of outer space, which receives the constant flow of infrared rays (heat radiation) given off by the upper atmosphere. All types of input energy eventually degrade into heat, which is then transported from earth to the cosmic sink as infrared radiation. The flow-through of energy leads to the organization of all the geospheres. That flux guarantees that chemical and physical organization will arise on the planet. It powers the cycles and relates the processes of each compartment to all the others. The manner in which it happens and the meaning of that energy-driven organization require further thought and study.

Many years ago and one island away, I wrote:

> The purpose of this book is to discuss and present evidence for the general thesis that *the flow of energy through a system acts to organize that system.* The motivation for this approach is biological and has its origins in an attempt to find a physical rationale for the extremely high degree of molecular order encountered in living systems. From the study of energy flow in a number of simple model systems, we shall attempt to demonstrate that the evolution of molecular order follows from known principles of present-day physics and does not require the introduction of new laws.

While I still agree with those words, the thoughts have now grown to more cosmic proportions. The universe and life are more closely related than had been realized.

My writing is over for the day. The librarian is eyeing the clock, and the bird of time has flown. It's a beautiful sunny afternoon, and I wander up Front Street oblivious of the tourists. I've become something of a local and am able to enter our sanctum sanctorum the Yacht Club. There, as I sit on the porch, it's nice to soak up the solar energy that is abundantly raining down on Lahaina. The arrival of an acquaintance leads to a game of pool, which serves as a reminder that my knowledge of conservation of momentum is greater than my ability to use that knowledge.

CHAPTER 7

Fitness and Design

On the spiritual odyssey to Lahaina, the first book that got packed in my movable library was *The Fitness of the Environment*, by Lawrence J. Henderson I've just reread that classic and would like to share the reasons for making this monograph my number-one material possession this year. This requires some historical perspective.

Looking for spiritual meaning within science is not a new idea. It was quite a popular intellectual activity in the eighteenth and nineteenth centuries, the period from Newton to Darwin. One of the best examples was the previously mentioned Bridgewater Treatises of the 1830s. These works on natural theology were written by eminent scientists with the purpose of showing evidence of the creator from a study of his creation.

This genre of literature had, at its core, a concept

called the argument from design, which implies that we need only examine the world around us to see that it must be the result of a creative intelligence rather than blind chance. However, the early adherents of this viewpoint always carried their argument at least one step further than its original logic and formed a chain of reasoning that went as follows: The observed world—implies: a creative intelligence—implies: a creator—implies: the Judeo-Christian God—implies: the established Church.

Those scientists who rejected the second and third or fourth implications in the sequence threw out the entire chain of reasoning, thus abandoning the first step, the argument from design, without giving it the consideration it deserves.

Following the work of Darwin as well as that of the nineteenth-century geologists, arguments found in the Bridgewater Treatises were dismissed as theological sophistry by many within the scientific community. The argument for the "creator" based on the designs of the "created" was totally rejected on the grounds that Darwinian fitness would result in the same remarkable adaptation of organisms to the laws of nature and boundary conditions of the planet. Scientists were locked in a bitter confrontation with established religions and instinctively turned their backs on all arguments suggestive of order or purpose. Yet the "will to survive," or the "thrust for fitness," that was introduced had a teleological content that evolutionary biologists such as Thomas Huxley and Ernst Haeckel chose to ignore. They replaced a religious metaphysics with a scientific metaphysics, but were unaware of the substitution.

In 1913, however, fitness and design were reexamined from a new scientific perspective. Distinguished Harvard professor of philosophy Lawrence J. Henderson wrote the profound and controversial book now sitting in front of me. Some sixty-four years had passed since Charles Darwin's *Origin of Species* had introduced the idea of "fitness" as the criterion of success in the struggle for survival. When new variations arose in the plant or animal world, they multiplied or perished depending on whether they were more or less adapted than the competition. Fitness was not an absolute concept but measured the relative survivals of different biological variants in a given habitat, under given conditions. Generations of evolutionists had already pointed out the somewhat circular nature of "survival of the fittest" as an argument for evolution, as we often lack criteria other than survival to measure fitness. Nevertheless, Darwin's ideas provided a unifying framework for biological thought, and by 1913 biology was thoroughly dominated by the theory of evolution.

Simultaneously with the rise and triumph of Darwinian evolution, physiology developed as a sophisticated science, using the understanding of physics and chemistry to explain the mechanisms of biological activity at every level. Henderson is a leader in that tradition. Indeed, some of his work on biophysical chemistry is still referred to today. He took a fresh view of fitness in terms of the new knowledge of physical chemistry and the ascendance of the atomic theory. He examined the argument from design, not from a theological perspective but from deep within science, using the constructs of matter, energy, space, and time. He wrote:

> But although Darwin's fitness involves that which fits and that which is fitted, or more correctly a reciprocal relationship, it has been the habit of biologists since Darwin to consider only the adaptations of the living organism to the environment. For them in fact, the environment, in its past, present, and future, has not been an independent variable, and it has not entered into any of the modern speculations to consider if by chance the material universe also may be subjected to laws which are in the largest sense important in organic evolution. Yet fitness there must be in environment as well as organism.

Henderson, writing in 1913, long before the establishment of global ecology, did not point out the extent to which organisms made the environment fit. That finding was later put forward by J. E. Lovelock, in his book *Gaia*, arguing that organisms influence and stabilize the environment. This extends Henderson's reasoning and provides one rationale for the fit between the two.

Henderson, arguing in scientific terms, urges us not only to examine the plasticity of organisms in adapting to the environment but also to examine those features of the environment that make life possible. To appreciate these insights, note that he wrote his book before the publication of Niels Bohr's quantum theory of the atom and four years before the modern theory of valence, telling how atoms are held together in molecules. Biochemistry was in its formative years, awaiting developments in organic chemistry. Most geologists believed that the continents and oceans were quite unchanging features of the earth's surface. Ecology was but a word and had not reached the status of a science. In this setting, Henderson set forth his views of fitness.

Matter as understood in 1913 consisted of the atoms of the periodic table, with their orderly repetition of chemical properties. The classification of the elements was based on atomic weights and the concept of atomic numbers was just being worked out. Energy was well understood, since the laws of classical thermodynamics were essentially complete when Henderson was still a student. Nuclear energy was not understood, the source of the sun's power was modestly noted in Henderson's books as unknown, and the concepts of space and time were still those of nineteenth-century physics.

The extent to which this physiologist's starting point was scientific rather than philosophical can be seen in his words: "But we can scarcely think that our present ideas are inadequate for our present purpose, or that, for life, matter will be other than the elements of the periodic classification, energy that set of quantities to which we apply the laws of thermodynamics, and Euclid."

Using physical criteria, Henderson stresses the biologist's view of the organism, a durable, complex form maintained by the flow-through of matter and energy. He is able to formulate the problem: "To what extent do the characteristics of matter and energy and the cosmic processes favor the existence of mechanisms that must be complex, highly regulated and provided with suitable matter and energy as food? If it shall appear that the fitness of the environment to fulfill these demands of life is great, we may then ask whether it is so great that we cannot reasonably assume it to be accidental, and finally we may inquire what manner of law is capable of explaining such fitness of the very nature of things."

The question is whether life with all its subtleties is some accidental property called into existence by events of blind chance or whether it is a more fundamental property of the world of nature. As we study the complex and interrelated aspects of planetary life, are we simply to attribute it all to random events, or are we to seek deep meanings about ourselves and the cosmos? Looking at the evidence, Henderson opted for the latter approach. So do I, but that commitment to meaning only becomes apparent after one spends some considerable effort looking into our understanding of the physics and chemistry of life and the biological applications.

With Henderson as mentor, one begins to explore early scientific fundamentals. These details, while not absolutely necessary to our approach, establish just how intelligent cosmic intelligence really is. The argument is far more persuasive when we can see all the pieces fitting into place. And the universe is most impressive in its detailed workings as well as in its broad scope.

The features looked at in *The Fitness of the Environment* are the solar system, the exceptional nature of water, the properties of carbon dioxide, the makeup and flow patterns of the oceans, and the chemistry of carbon, hydrogen, and oxygen compounds. After a detailed analysis of these subjects in the light of the science of his day, Henderson focused on the question of whether the earth is uniquely suited to life or whether other environments might prove equally habitable. He gave special attention to the occurrence of great quantities of water and carbon dioxide on the outside of the solid crust of an astronomical body. After a rather long and detailed discussion of the special properties of the earth, it was then concluded that "the above catalogued natural characteristics of the environment promote and favor complexity, regulation, and metabolism, the three fundamental characteristics of life."

Henderson assured himself that his treatment had been exhaustive, no important physical features had been neglected, and no other chemicals would suffice, no other combination of elements from the periodic table would work so well. He finally concluded that life is somehow a property of the evolving universe and "that genetic and evolutionary properties, both cosmic and biological when considered in certain aspects, constitute a single orderly development that yields results not merely contingent, but resembling those which in human action we recognize as purposeful."

Henderson's line of reasoning started with the then-current theories and observations of science. He fully accepted the approach of his time and then asked: "Can we by analyzing these results formulate a metatheory that gives us a more extended vision?" After answering this question with a yes, he began to tentatively grope for that metatheory that would tell us more about ourselves and our place in the universe. Knowledge of the material world need not alienate us from more spiritual thoughts; it can indeed guide us to such thoughts.

It is now more than seventy years since the great physiologist set forth his views. Our knowledge of biology and biochemistry is vastly more detailed and extends down to the atomic and electronic level of organization. Our understanding of the planet and the universe are radically different from anything envisioned in the early part of the century. With all these scientific advances, our sense of the reciprocal relationship, or mutual fitness, seems to grow deeper and more profound. The puzzle now has many more parts, but the way in which they fit together remains just as striking.

To some degree, the approach in these pages is a re-examination of Henderson's ideas in the light of modern science and as modified by Lovelock's ideas about the environment's being influenced by organisms. I share Henderson's feeling that the remarkable reciprocity between organism and environment cannot be ignored either by scientists or philosophers.

The Fitness of the Environment is not widely known among contemporary scientists, many of whom have renounced purpose from a methodological point of view. Yet this rejection has likely been premature. My copy of Henderson's book is staying right here in the main cabin as an incentive to move ahead in this business.

CHAPTER 8

Propaedeutics

At a certain level one describes life in terms of its elemental components; at the other extreme one deals with trees, birds, insects, bacteria, and the fascinating flora and fauna found in the array of habitats of our planet. These two levels, the molecular and the ecological, refer to the same life, and one of our tasks in the "earth, air, fire, and water" approach is to show how they are related. At the ecological level the biosphere interacts with the other geochemical spheres, but fitness in the macroscopic domain must ultimately reflect events at the molecular level. A fascinating feature of earth is the well-matched character of large-scale global processes and detailed molecular interactions. It is this beautiful match that is leading us on to some of our philosophical thoughts, and appreciating it requires some understanding of scientific fundamentals.

One of my all-time favorite words is "propaedeutics." It gets me into a lot of trouble, because university faculty members tend to get angry with someone who uses a word they don't know. It's not their fault; it's just that they are, by definition, superbly well educated, so that if you employ unfamiliar vocabulary, you are doing something tricky. The reason I nevertheless like "propaedeutics" is that it means "the underlying fundamentals necessary to understand any subject," those basic ideas that make possible all further comprehension. It's a powerful word, promising the possibility of rational development of thought.

But before discussing some foundations of modern science for use in subsequent discussions, I would like to "talk story," as some harbormates are wont to say.

Recently a conference of European theologians speculated on the problems of birth control. While there was a strong opposition to mechanical methods, a much more favorable attitude was developing toward the pill. A young cleric arose and said, "Gentlemen, we will become the laughingstock of the century if we maintain that chemistry will allow you to enter heaven, while physics will send you to hell." Had that man of the cloth been a man of the lab coat, his argument probably would have been phrased in terms of the difference between the large-scale macroscopic concepts used in designing mechanical contraceptives and the small-scale submicroscopic molecular view of nature employed in the chemical pharmaceutical approach to birth control. Those two outlooks dominate modern science, and the relations between them provide the connectivity so important in the choice of theoretical approaches.

The approach of modern science is called reductionism, the attempt to understand phenomena at one level of organization in terms of mechanisms at an underlying level of organization. A geologist studying rocks tries to reduce their structure to the crystalline domains out of which they are made. The crystals are analyzed in terms of the atoms of oxygen, silicon, aluminum, and other constituent elements. The arrangement of the atoms is studied in terms of nuclei and electrons and the quantum mechanical rules that govern their interactions. If one wanted to go a step further, the nuclei could be studied in terms of elementary particles. But there is a limit to which reductionism is usually carried, and most of the understanding of macroscopic phenomena is reduced to the electrons and nuclei of atoms.

These scientific relations show how superbly the world is designed. In addition, scientific views such as quantum mechanics must ultimately influence our philosophical outlook. The earlier founders of quantum theory wrote philosophical books explaining the new science to the world of humanistic thought. Atomism and quantum theory profoundly color the world view of the twentieth century.

From the present perspective, the most exciting feature is the way that atomic laws generate a large-scale system, giving rise to earth, air, fire, and water. Things have to be just right at the submicroscopic level to generate the universe we know and love. And they are just right!

The next step is to discuss those atomic constructs propaedeutic to modern geology and biology. Atomic theory dates back to the Greeks and Democritus' doctrine in 400 B.C.E., although its final universal acceptance is a twentieth-century happening. Ludwig Boltzmann, who, at the turn of the century, was the foremost advocate of the atomic theory of matter, died in 1906. The depressive state that led to his suicide was thought to have been partially caused by the failure of some colleagues to accept his views on the reality of atoms. Alas, he acted too hastily, for a few years later his theories were completely triumphant. The moral is, Don't despair; you might just be ahead of your time.

Before the atomic view became universally accepted, chemists were aware that all matter was made up of approximately ninety elements, and the Russian Dmitry Mendeleyev had shown that by approximately placing the elements (according to atomic weight) on a two-dimensional chart, remarkable periodicities could be seen in the chemical properties. The periodic table, which now hangs as a decorative chart in every chemistry classroom, is the clue to an orderliness in the structural properties of the atomic constituents of all matter. Once Boltzmann's advocacy of the reality of atoms was accepted, it was possible to return to Democritus' view that elements differed because they were composed of fundamental particles of different structures. To keep the record straight, it should be mentioned that the chemist Mendeleyev, the biologist Darwin, and the physicist Clausius, who formulated the second law of thermodynamics, were all contemporaries, individually and collectively participating in the enormous upheaval of society's view of itself and its universe that marked the mid-nineteenth century. Their ideas continue to reverberate.

The twentieth century brought the unfolding of the science of nuclear physics and the discovery that atoms consist of small, dense, positively charged nuclei, surrounded by an equivalent negative electrical charge in electrons. Chemical properties are due to the arrangement of electrons, and the periodic table reflects the ordering of these tiny electrical units. Niels Bohr suggested that electrons circle the nuclei in the same manner that planets orbit the sun; the difference being that all the elecrons are identical in charge and mass, and only certain orbits are allowable, corresponding to quantized energy levels. The number and distribution of electrons among possible orbits then determine all chemical properties of an atom.

At the turn of the century physicist Max Planck suggested that light energy could be emitted or absorbed by atoms only in certain discrete amounts called quanta. Albert Einstein had formulated a law governing the behavior of electrons released in photoelectric experiments involving light falling on metal surfaces and electrons coming out of the metal. An understanding of this phenomenon required that light energy be quantized. The connectivity criterion, so important to deep theory, was coming into play through evidence from many branches of physics and chemistry and was focusing on the idea that energy and energy change at the atomic level were discrete quantities. This was an unexpected result, starting from classical large-scale physics, and one which caused wonder. Further surprises were in store.

The first novelty came when attempts were made to improve the Bohr theory and provide a detailed view of atoms other than hydrogen, that is, for atoms containing more than one electron. These efforts, along with new data on the scattering of electrons from crystals, led to modern quantum mechanics, a deeply mathematical and not very intuitive theory about how electrons behave in atoms. Quantum mechanics involves an unusual set of constructs that are justified by the metaphysical criteria and the loop of verification, that is, they are accepted because they work in providing the right answers. The theory elegantly explains and predicts sense data or experimental results. It does a better job of such explanation than any other present-day theory that meets the same criteria for scientific validity. In the process of achieving this goal, quantum mechanics asserts that an electron sometimes acts like a wave and sometimes like a particle. It is impossible to measure precisely, at the same time, the location and speed of an atomic particle. It is impossible to know at any time exactly where an electron is in an atom; the best we can do is to give the probability of finding it at each point.

There is a certain strangeness in all this. Everyday intuitions that proved valuable in large-scale physics don't hold at the atomic level; that domain has its own laws. These features troubled the founders of quantum mechanics. There was an outpouring of philosophy by most of the major figures in the development of the new science. They were so startled by the implications of what they had done that they felt it necessary to justify their work to a wider public. Einstein until his death refused to accept the probabilistic nature of quantum theory. He would say, "God does not play dice with the universe." Erwin Schrödinger, one of the founders of the theory, responded by moving toward the perennial philosophy of Aldous Huxley and then to Vedantic mysticism. That theme of relating physics to Oriental philosophy continues today in the popular realm in *The Tao of Physics* and *The Dancing Wu Li Masters*. Max Planck and Werner Heisenberg wrote humanistic quasi-religious works stemming from the new physics. Wolfgang Pauli worked with Jung on psychology with a mystical flavor, and Walter Elsasser began a search for biogenic principles. Eugene Wigner responded by developing a mentalist philosophy that is accepted by a large number of quantum theoreticians. Never have such a gifted group of physicists plunged into so many philosophical traditions to seek meaning.

Unless one studies the history of science of the first half of the twentieth century in some detail, it is difficult to grasp the magnitude of the alterations in thought patterns. Nothing like this occurs at any other period in history. The changes came at such a rapid pace that there was no time to absorb new knowledge by letting a rising generation replace the old. This accelerated pace of ideas seems to be with us still, and in new fields of artificial intelligence and molecular genetics events are following with such alacrity that it may take decades or longer to sort out philosophical consequences of the new knowledge.

There has always been a flow of thought from science to philosophy to the world of political action and public policy. We first try to understand the world by the objective criteria available to us. We then move to the deeper meaning in that understanding. Finally there is the attempt to go from deep understanding to action, to establish a society that embodies the philosophical first principles.

I learned this as an undergraduate sitting in F. S. C. Northrop's class on the philosophy of science. He said:

> All these considerations indicate that differences in ideology in the social sciences and the humanities are rooted in differences in the philosophies underlying these ideologies and that the philosophies in turn are connected with the results of scientific inquiry and are always regarded by the people who hold them as called for by the scientific knowledge which they take into account. Put more concretely, what this means is that many people are impressed by the facts of their experience which fall within their attention. From these facts they derive, consciously or unconsciously, a specific scientific generation or theory. The analysis of this theory, after the manner in which Locke analyzed the physics of Galilei and Newton, brings out an explicit philosophy. In terms of this philosophy they define their economic, political, religious and other humanistic doctrines and attendant social institutions. The good state is the state which permits the person to be the kind of person which such a scientifically verified philosophy designates a person to be.

What is distinctive about the twentieth century is that the same individuals who developed the science also tried to search out the philosophical and social consequences. The science itself is sufficiently difficult that there has been a lag in philosophers outside of science acquiring sufficient understanding to seek deeper meaning. We are now in a state of confusion because there has been insufficient time to develop the social consequences of quantum-mechanical relativistic man.

The way in which the founders of the new physics responded by philosophizing is a good example of how views of natural science profoundly influence our concepts of a personal and religious nature. The scientific community is a bit embarrassed, but I don't see why. Our varying descriptions apply to the same world. It is the identical universe for the poet, the theologian, and the physicist. If they communicate insights to each other, we should rejoice; ultimately their views must merge or we shall have a fragmented understanding. Surely the first of the two possibilities seems more desirable. Quantum mechanics has not fully worked its way from the ivory tower into popular philosophy. It has been a mind-shaking experience for those involved in the original discoveries. It is not possible to predict what the effect will be when the results of this physics become a part of the general culture. They will be profound, and I look forward to them.

Since quantum mechanics is so extraordinarily successful in explaining so much of physics, chemistry, and biology, it is clear that it must be included in our more general view of the real world, even if we feel damned uncomfortable about our ability to get an intuitive feel for it. If this is disturbing, even more so did it bother those great thinkers who produced the structure and were then awestruck by their creation.

One is reminded of the Greek legend of the sculptor Pygmalion, who fashioned a statue of a maiden. The Goddess of Love brought the statue to life, Pygmalion named here Galatea, and they were married. So physicists seem wedded to the product of their creative genius. Quantum mechanics has become part of our lives, a gift of the gods that we accept in our search for truth as Pygmalion accepted Galatea in his search for love.

I hope this story makes quantum mechanics more acceptable for social conversation. If the equations lack the warmth of Galatea, they certainly possess great beauty when viewed by physicists, and they have been fertile in producing another generation of scientific understanding.

When solving the equations of quantum mechanics for an atom, one finds that the appropriate description of the state of an electron is in terms of four numbers. The necessity of four such quantities is related to the four-dimensional space-time of relativity. The two great physical theories of our century are combined, and the numbers completely describe the electron within the allowable limits of the theory. The theory also necessitates that these numbers can only have integral values, such as 0, 1, 2, 3, 4, 5, etc. Thus $(4,3,2,0)$, $(3,1,0,0)$, and $(2,1,1,1)$ describe three different states of an electron. These integers are called quantum numbers because for each set of four there exists a discrete quantized energy value. From classical physics we should expect that all the electrons in an atom would be in the lowest possible energy states. At this point the next surprise enters.

A rather astounding law of nature discovered by Wolfgang Pauli in 1925 states that *no two electrons in an atom can have the same set of four quantum numbers*. The first conclusion from that simple-sounding statement is the prediction of all the regularities seen in the periodic table of the elements. As the number of electrons builds up in succeeding elements, each added electron must be assigned to an unoccupied quantum state; it is excluded from the quantum states that are already filled. That occupancy rule establishes the chemical properties of atoms, which are determined by the numbers of electrons in incomplete shells. The very idea of shells comes from the grouping of electrons according to the Pauli rule. In short, all aspects of chemical structure follow from those considerations.

Without studying quantum theory it is difficult to grasp the profound importance of the Pauli principle. Yet it is so vital in understanding the nature of the world around us that the concept should be available to a wider public, and I am trying.

The other day, on the Yacht Club sundeck I was lunching and discussing a book review with a friend who had kindly agreed to critique it for me. He was

objecting to my use of the phrase "Pauli exclusion principle" because of unfamiliarity with the concept. His
comments served as a reminder that only a few weeks
ago, an editor of a popular science magazine had blue-
penciled a reference to that same principle of physics
on the ground that the concept would be unfamiliar to
most readers. A quick survey was in order, and I spotted
an acquaintance with a degree in zoology. "Jack, have
you ever heard of the Pauli exclusion principle?"
"What's that?" was the reply.

Before going further, I must opine that the physical
theory under discussion is one of the important scientific
discoveries of the twentieth century. To quote the
editors of Dr. Pauli's *Collected Scientific Papers*: "His
exclusion principle, for which he received the Nobel
award in 1945, is one of the main pillars of quantum
mechanics. It is the cornerstone upon which rests all
quantum mechanical understanding of the structure of
matter." I'll add that the exclusion principle provides
the most solid basis available for our comprehending
much of chemistry and biochemistry.

That raises some questions: Who was Pauli? What is
the nature of his exclusion principle? Why has such an
important relation of physics been unknown not only to
the public but even to the scientifically trained?

The second question first. The Pauli principle, while
easy to state, is conceptually deep, dark, different, and
difficult. It has a character unlike most other laws of
nature, which makes it hard to comprehend. Its description requires an amount of background in atomic

physics. The result of my brief survey at the Yacht Club and man-in-the-street interviews is that most teachers simply avoid Dr. Pauli's result. They find it too difficult to teach. But surely neglecting something so important is a problem in contemporary science education. That notion ennobles the task of answering the first two of the three questions we have asked.

Wolfgang Pauli was a man of genius and accompanying eccentricities. Born in 1900 in Vienna, Austria, he was the son of a colloid chemist and godson of Ernst Mach, a man whose opposition to the atomic theory led him to numerous conflicts with Boltzmann. Young Pauli was five years old when Albert Einstein brought out the first paper on special relativity. A few years later, young Wolfgang, bored with high school, would sit in class secretly reading Einstein's work by hiding it within his textbook. That method of learning paid off handsomely, for when he reached the mature age of twenty, he wrote a two-hundred-page encyclopedia article on relativity theory, which has remained until now a standard exposition of that difficult subject.

Five years after completing his relativity paper, Pauli was engaged in a study of atomic structure and the newly emerging quantum physics. Following Bohr's planetary theory of atoms, more elaborate formulations developed that required the orbit of each electron to be specified by three quantum numbers, integers corresponding to the three dimensions of ordinary space. Experiments with atoms in magnetic fields indicated that a more complete description of electron orbits required the addition of a fourth quantum number related to the time dimension. An examination of a large body of experimental information then led Pauli to conclude that no two electrons in an atom can have the same set of four quantum numbers.

In 1928, three years after the discovery of the exclusion principle, Pauli was appointed professor at the Technical College in Zurich, Switzerland, where he remained until his death in 1958. He was charismatic in the physics community, and it was always his hope that physics would indicate the mysterious harmony of God and nature. In 1952 he coauthored with psychoanalyst Carl Jung a book called *The Explanation of Nature and Psyche*.

The exclusion principle of the remarkable Dr. Pauli has a character different from the usual laws of physics, which require a system to assume the configuration of lowest energy consistent with external conditions at the boundaries. Consider the lithium atom, with three electrons. The first two occupy a filled shell. The third electron is excluded from that inner orbit, since there are no other sets of four quantum numbers available that specify an electron in that shell. The electron therefore goes into an outer shell even though the lowest energy value would correspond to having all the electrons in the lowest energy state. It is as if the third electron knew what the other two were doing. That kind of mentalistic character of the Pauli rule is what renders it so strange and difficult to comprehend. It is as if electrons were sensing their environment by other than strictly energetic means—a curious kind of perception. Philosopher of science Henry Margenau describes the

Pauli principle as "a way of understanding why entities show in their togetherness laws of behavior different from the laws which govern them in isolation." He feels that because of that character, the exclusion rule may form a bridge between physics and biology, perhaps between matter and mind. It illuminates our understanding of why the whole might be different from the sum of the parts.

I hope to have convinced you that the exclusion principle should be part of the background of every educated man, woman, and child. It's right up there in importance with the second law of thermodynamics, and certainly everyone at the Yacht Club must have heard of the second law, although some are presently having problems with Archimedes' principle of buoyancy. But that's another story.

Let's review the bidding; the principle we are discussing is not energetic but informational, with a mental aspect about it. Earlier laws of physics could always be put in terms of energy relationships. The Pauli principle is a physical law, but of an entirely different character. Because of it, energy minimization no longer applies in atoms. In addition, if no two electrons can have the same set of quantum numbers, how does one electron know the quantum numbers of the other electrons? The principle can be derived from deeper symmetry conditions, but it always goes beyond purely energetic considerations. Exclusion introduces a property of electrons in aggregate that is not possessed by single electrons. Without the Pauli principle, matter would tend to be just homogeneous stuff; with it, there emerges the potential for all the exquisite chemical order seen in earth, air, fire, and water.

Quantum mechanics' second surprise is the depth and range of its explanatory power once the exclusion rule is applied. First, from systematically building up the set of allowed electron configurations, the entire periodic table becomes predictable from first principles. That information-packed table of the elements hanging in every chemistry classroom can be rationally understood. In addition, the explanation of the covalent bonding of atoms also emerges. Since knowledge of chemical compounds follows from the periodic table and the rules of bond formation, molecular structures can be understood and predicted. One law of nature of an informational character makes the difference between an inert, rather structureless world and the exquisite molecular order that surrounds us. This kind of finding gets one really excited in thinking about the creative intelligence inherent in the laws of nature, and gives us, as well, the ability to ultimately comprehend that intelligence. As a scientist, I find it embarrassing to be a cheerleader for a mysterious cosmic intelligence, but that seems to be where I'm heading. In any case, the laws governing the lithosphere, hydrosphere, atmosphere, and biosphere are all crucially dependent on the Pauli principle. That rule may also have something to say about the mind-body problem.

The astounding success of the Pauli relation in showing how chemical structure can emerge from physics leads us to inquire if a similar principle might explain the rise of biological order from chemistry. At this point the question is purely speculative, though fascinating. At least the existence of one such relationship makes it possible to ask about others. Such an undiscovered principle, if it existed, would be biogenic but would not be any more vitalistic than the Pauli principle. It would simply be another example of a physical principle that emerges at a given level of complexity. *Vitalism* is an epithet that biologists use to describe other people's theories about life that cannot immediately be derived from existing physical principles. This is too restrictive a point of view.

If I seem overly optimistic about the potential of the laws of physics, there is good reason. I have just replaced the entire dimmer circuit for the compass and knot-meter lights, and they are working. Since the job proceeded entirely on first principles, it gave me renewed confidence in the basic laws of electricity. Hydrodynamics having been reestablished by my having replaced the diaphragm on the bilge pump, an entire range of scientific discipline appears, for today in any case, to be in good shape.

While things are looking up, we had better move on to the laws of radiation. They are necessary to understanding the atmosphere and the relation between the earth and the sun. Most of the energy that powers processes on our planet arrives in the form of radiation, the amount and type of which is also part of planetary fitness.

All bodies radiate heat to their surroundings and absorb heat radiation from their surroundings. We live in a sea of electromagnetic energy, which is usually undetected since we are emitting approximately as much as we are absorbing. On a chilly, windless night our exposed skin feels cold because it is giving off more heat to the surroundings than it is taking in, a point I became icily aware of a while back when I had to camp out on a mountaintop above eleven thousand feet, where the greenhouse effect of the atmosphere was providing little protection against heat loss.

Before the turn of the century it was determined that the amount of radiation emitted by a unit area of surface of any object is proportional to the fourth power of its absolute temperature (amount emitted = constant $\times$ T $\times$ T $\times$ T $\times$ T). The absolute temperature scale is a method of measuring that quantity from absolute zero, where all molecular motion ceases. Numerically it is equal to centigrade temperature plus 273. The amount absorbed is proportional to the fourth power of the absolute temperature of the surroundings. The relationship is named the Stefan-Boltzmann law. Josef Stefan, a physicist, discovered it experimentally and his colleague and student Boltzmann devised a theoretical explanation. Note that the name of Ludwig Boltzmann keeps popping up. That remarkable scientist was responsible for much of our understanding of the physical world, and we keep encountering his contributions whenever we go back to first principles.

A fourth-power law, while seemingly innocent enough mathematically, is really very powerful. It means that if we double the temperature of an object (from, let us say, room temperature [300° absolute] to 600° absolute), we increase the amount of radiation given off by sixteenfold (2 × 2 × 2 × 2). By the time we get to an object like the sun, which is nineteen times the temperature of the earth, a unit area of surface is giving off 140,000 times as much energy per unit area. These radiation laws assume importance when we consider why our planet is not a frigid waste or a crisp cinder.

This universal type of electromagnetic energy given off by all objects is named black-body radiation and is characterized by a spectral distribution as well as a total quantity. The spectral distribution is the amount of light given off at each wavelength. We tend to think of spectra in terms of the color of visible radiation, but it also includes infrared (heat), ultraviolet, X rays, and radio waves. On a frequency scale, the various radiations can be arranged as follows:

	Gamma Rays ↑	(Highest Frequency)
	X Rays	
	Ultraviolet	
	Blue	
Wavelength	Yellow	Frequency
	Red	
	Infrared	
	Microwave	
↓	Radio Frequency	(Lowest Frequency)

Frequency and wavelength are related quantities; as one goes up, the other goes down. In the wave theory of light we have the relation:

Frequency × wavelength = velocity of propagation

Since Dr. Einstein has convinced us that the velocity of light is a universal constant, frequency and wavelength are inverse quantities.

Different kinds of radiation have very different effects when they impinge on matter. The low-frequency infrared, microwave, and radio waves simply warm things up. The highly energetic gamma rays and X rays break up chemical structures and tear molecules apart. The intermediate visible radiation (red, yellow, and blue) energizes molecules without destroying them so that they can undergo photochemical reactions. Most of the sunlight falling on our planet is of this intermediate range. In an important, energetic way it is the right stuff for photosynthesis.

We can, using a formula by Planck, calculate the energy per unit area given off by objects of different temperatures at different wavelengths. The total energy of all wavelengths is the quantity that varies with the fourth power of the temperature. The frequency at which the maximum amount of energy is emitted is experimentally found to vary directly with the temperature. This is called the displacement law and enables us to measure the temperature of a distant object by analyzing its light spectroscopically and measuring which frequency range has the greatest energy. I'm reminded of a song from a marvelous science-teaching record. My children used to sing it and the words that keep reverberating through my head are "The color of a star, you can be sure, is mainly due to its temperature." Yes, it is. Beyond that thought, there is the sense of wonderment that we can measure the temperature of objects vast distances from our planet, vaster than most of us can contemplate.

The theoretical understanding of the spectral distribution of black-body radiation was the beginning of quantum mechanics. The history of radiation theory from Josef Stefan to Max Planck is one of those fascinating epochs that began with careful measurements and ended in a theory that has revolutionized our view of the world. That often is the way of science, but rarely are the changes of perspective so radical.

While we're enjoying the laws of physics, it's time to extend our perspective to the size of atoms and the chaos that exists in the molecular domain. How big is an atom? Let's start with the engine block on the Atomic 4. It's about two feet long and therefore the length occupied by about two billion iron atoms laid end to end. Perhaps we should try a smaller object, like the top of the spark plug, which is about twenty million atomic diameters from one side to the other. The smallest thing I have on board is some 2.5-mil wire in the toolbox. I don't know how it got there or what it's used for, but Captain Bobbie doesn't like to throw things away. In any case, the radius of this wire would involve about two hundred thousand copper atoms next to each other in a row. To deal with something smaller, I have my small pocket microscope. Looking at the ruler, I can see the lines on the metric scale that mark out the millimeters. The lines themselves are about a tenth of a millimeter, and there are specks of ink about a tenth the width of the line, or a hundredth of a millimeter, which would correspond to a linear arrangement of about sixty thousand carbon atoms. Back in the laboratory the smallest thing I normally look at with my 980-power microscope are tiny bacterialike cells that are about fifteen hundred atomic diameters across. Atoms are small, but not so tiny that one can't see their effects.

Back in 1827, a botanist by the name of Robert Brown was looking through his microscope at some very tiny pollen grains in water. They bounded about in a very irregular way, a feature that Brown soon found was universal for all very tiny objects suspended in fluids. Some seventy-five years later, Einstein and others fully explained this Brownian motion as the fluctuation effect of unequal numbers of fluid molecules bouncing off each side of the suspended object. The resultant bouncing around is a tangible, visible result of the molecular nature of matter. If we cannot see atoms and molecules, we can see the statistical result of their motion, and this led to the measurement of atomic dimensions from Brownian motion by the French physicist Jean-Baptiste Perrin in 1913.

The phenomenon discovered by Brown is evidence that molecules are in constant motion that is random with respect to speed and direction. Indeed, absolute temperature is dependent on the average velocity of atoms in any substance. If we could view matter at a molecular level, we would see molecules moving, twisting, and vibrating in an endless erratic dance. Heat is the large-scale manifestation of that random molecular motion.

This small-scale randomness leads us to ask how the beautifully precise molecular structures of biology that we see in all the plants and animals around us can be produced in the face of constant chaotic disordering. It's as if a craftsman doing very fine, delicate work has his shop in a building being constantly shaken by earthquakes. That question about order and disorder was first asked in this way by physicist Erwin Schrödinger in 1942. The answers are not all in, but it's something biophysicists are beginning to understand. For the moment any local interest in biology is more immediately taken up by shouting about a three-hundred-pound marlin being brought in at the gas dock. It's hard to resist taking a look.

The marlin weights over three hundred pounds when hoisted up on the dock scales, and that provides a fitting contrast to the submicroscopic perspectives of organisms. Life as viewed by modern molecular biologists is understood in terms of the basic concepts of physics and chemistry. Henderson also had looked to those sciences and started from the fundamentals of space, time, matter, and energy. Space and time can be taken as givens for biology, although cosmologists now require a much deeper look at even those aspects of physics. We are able to focus on matter and energy and would be inclined to add an additional quantity, information. Although information does not exist apart from matter and energy, it represents, in terms of the Pauli principle and rules of quantum mechanics, a sufficiently different aspect of those fundamental quantities that it should be examined separately. Information allows us to focus on the molecular organization of the atoms of living systems.

The material of our earth-based biological systems is made up largely of carbon, hydrogen, nitrogen, oxygen, phosphorus, and sulfur, which are recalled by the mnemonic CHNOPS, pronounced "schnops." If we were to deal only with lumps of carbon, sulfur, and phosphate, along with water and gaseous nitrogen, we would not be concerned with information but would simply use the large-scale laws of chemistry and thermodynamics. In living cells, however, the atoms of CHNOPS are assembled in exquisitely precise molecular structures, such as proteins, nucleic acids, fats, and carbohydrates. These macromolecules are themselves delicately arrayed into more complex entities, the cell's organelles. In these highly ordered systems information measures the specificity of molecular states (positions of the atoms) of living organisms compared to all possible states. The more precisely a system needs to be specified, the higher its information measure. The ability to maintain and reproduce order at the atomic level is one of the defining properties of life as we know it.

The detailed understanding of the processes of molecular biology make it difficult to conceive of any life that is not made up of parts that are highly ordered at the atomic level. Growth consists of taking chemicals from a disordered solution phase in the environment and incorporating the atoms into precise structures.

Matter in the biologist's sense is best viewed in terms of the periodic table and those ninety or so naturally occurring elements that make up the earth's surface. The ordering of matter, although constrained by the Pauli exclusion principle, requires the continuous expenditure of energy; for systems left to themselves will eventually end up in a maximum-entropy, minimum-information configuration, which is inconsistent with life. That statement is a further content of the celebrated second law of thermodynamics.

Energy enters the biosphere largely through the flow of photons from the sun to the earth and leaves as heat, thermal energy radiated as infrared photons into the vastness of outer space. That flow-through of solar power organizes the planet at both the microscopic and macroscopic levels. The second flow-through of organizing energy comes from radioactive decay within the earth itself. The two sources are responsible for almost all of the organized features in the world around us.

Thermal energy, measured by the temperature of an object, has a special status in thermodynamics in all processes ranging from chemical reactions to nuclear fusion. The temperature concept bridges the gulf from the macroscopic level, where it is defined in terms of the efficiency of heat engines, to the submicroscopic domain, where it is shown to be a measure of the average kinetic energy of atoms. Understanding the energy concept over the size range from engines to atoms has been one of the triumphs of classical physics. The scientific development of temperature measurement began with the primitive notions of hot and cold in everyday life. Temperature is now a precisely defined parameter of first importance in physics and chemistry, and interpretation exists even at the atomic level.

In any piece of matter all the atoms are in constant random motion. This view of the microscopic domain goes back more than two hundred years to Count Rumford's studying the heating of metal during the boring of cannon. In this kinetic-theory explanation, gas and liquid molecules wander through the fluid in a kind of drunkard's walk, and atoms of solids vibrate around their fixed positions and occasionally break away. There is constant energy exchange among atoms by collision and radiation, and the energy of any molecule is continually varying. The kinetic energy that an atom possesses because of all its random motion is measured in terms of the square of the speed with which it is moving.

The rates of chemical reactions depend critically on the temperature. Chemical change requires a collision between molecules that are sufficiently energetic to activate a rearrangement of atoms. The higher the temperature the faster molecules move, the more frequently they collide, and the more likely that a collision will be sufficiently energetic to cause a chemical change. As a result, chemical-reaction rates tend to increase rapidly with rising temperature. For a number of biological processes the rates increase approximately twofold for every ten-degree rise in temperature. This effect applies to such different processes as the chirping rate of crickets and the speed of enzymatic reactions.

The temperature range for most organic reactions is 200 to 600 degrees Kelvin ($-73°$ C to $327°$ C). Below this limit, reactions tend to proceed so slowly as to be of little interest on an ordinary time scale. Above this range many organic molecules become unstable. At higher temperatures chemical forms other than molecules become important. These include free radicals, ions, and multiply-ionized atoms and molecules. Above 1,000 degrees absolute, few molecules are found, and matter is characterized by atoms and ions. At even higher temperatures, samples are completely ionized and exist in states called dense plasmas. Temperature is still proportional to the average kinetic energy per particle, but the particles of interest are now nuclei and electrons.

At very high temperatures the nuclei become sufficiently energetic to react with one another by thermonuclear processes such as fusion, which releases additional energy. This kind of nuclear reaction deep within the cores of stars supplies the great quantities of energy radiated by these bodies. The sun is our nearest example. Research on fusion reactions involves an attempt to utilize this process to provide energy for everyday applications in running power plants. From the perspective of earth, air, fire, and water we are most interested in two temperature ranges, the chemical at the low end and the nuclear at the high end. The former helps us to narrow in on a meaningful temperature range for life, and the latter defines the ultimate solar mechanism for powering much of our planet.

Underlying all the laws of nature that we have been talking about and propaedeutic to them is the physicists' world of quarks, baryons, leptons, and the entire range of fundamental particles and fields. This level of description has its own vocabulary and its own sense of what is fundamental. In any case, the elementary particles give rise to nuclei, electrons, and their interactions. At the level of geology and biology, a description at the atomic level seems sufficient to understand most processes. We pursue our inquiry at that level but are constantly prepared to move back to fundamentals or ahead to a higher hierarchical level, such as the Pauli principle or beyond. In seeking philosophical perspective, every branch of science must be given its full weight.

CHAPTER 9

An Unusual Substance

I am back thinking about the "ancient mariner" again. There is a member of the dock community, an old drifter whose scrawny arms and deep-set eyes could have provided a model for the poet Coleridge. He is homeless, and in the early morning I have seen him sleeping on the ground in back of the public toilets; but that is another story. What has caught my attention at present is the line "Water, water, everywhere." It is time to think of the next geosphere, yet impossible to do so until we focus on both the large-scale and molecular properties of water. It is not only the hydrosphere that concerns us, for the atmosphere and living matter are both critically influenced by the properties of water. It all leads up to some tricky questions. Is it possible to conceive of life on a very dry planet? Can we envision living systems that are not largely made up of water or is life such a specific molecular property that liquid water is an absolute requirement? The answers to these may be limited by our imagination, but they are heavily influenced by the remarkable properties of water and the roles it plays. The only life we know is so adapted to water as a solvent, as a chemical component, and as a habitat that we find it difficult to think in other terms.

In his *Fitness of the Environment* Professor Henderson argues that the properties of water are so truly unique among all possible compounds that the fitness of life to water and water to life are reciprocal. He picks a group of important properties promoting fitness in the environment, and these deserve some discussion.

In getting adequately excited about the properties of water, I imagine myself going up to W. C. Fields in a bar and trying to convince him of the importance of the stuff. You will recall that the comedian is said to have remarked: "I never drink water; fish copulate in it." He didn't actually say "copulate," but I'm not one of those modern writers who throw around four-letter words with abandon, even in quotes. In any case, I would block his exit with a barstool and begin.

Water among all substances has one of the highest heat capacities, which is the amount of heat required to change the temperature by one degree. As a result, organisms and oceans, which are made up largely of water, are stabilized against rapid changes of temperature that may take place in the surroundings. In return, oceans act to moderate the temperature of the entire planet, keeping it from too rapid fluctuations.

Water among all common substances has one of the highest latent heats of melting, that is, a large quantity of energy is required to melt a given amount of ice. It also means that substantial heat must be given off in freezing a given quantity of water. In cold weather the temperature of systems is stabilized near the freezing point, and transitions between liquid and solid states are gradual. I'm told that some Eskimos heat their igloos by bringing in buckets of water acquired by chopping holes in the ice. The latent heat of melting keeps the interior from going below the freezing point. When the water freezes they discard the cake of ice and bring in more water.

The latent heat of vaporization is another quantity that has a high value. It is the energy necessary to vaporize a given amount of water. Its magnitude keeps the oceans from evaporating away and leaves the planet mostly covered by water. High latent heat also makes sweating a good way to keep the body from getting too hot, since large amounts of energy go into evaporating the sweat.

Water is peculiar among substances in undergoing a large expansion on freezing. Thus ice is 10 percent less dense than water at the freezing point, and icebergs and ice cubes float with a 10 percent tip sticking out of the liquid. As a result, bodies of water freeze from the top down rather than from the bottom up. This has a large effect on planetary weather and the survival of aquatic life in winter.

Related to the expansion on freezing is a property of water known as the anomalous expansion before freezing. Most liquids get denser and denser as the temperature drops. This is also true for water down to 4° C, when the trend reverses and it gets progressively less dense until it expands on freezing. Thus the lowest layer in a cold body of water is not the coldest but a 4° zone that stabilizes the bottom.

Water is clearly an excellent solvent for all kinds of molecules that show some distribution of electrical charge. This property is most important in the role of water as the primary material in the cell responsible for keeping in solution the variety of molecules necessary for cellular activity. The solvent power also plays a role in the hydrological cycle, in which the rainfall leaches the soil and carries dissolved molecules to the ocean.

The dielectric constant of a material measures the extent to which embedded electrical charges separate in an electrical field. As a result, in substances of high dielectric constant, such as water, the electrical field drops off very rapidly around charged particles. This is a favorable condition for salts dissolving in a liquid and also for dissolved acids and bases dissociating into charged ions.

Surface tension is the energy required to increase the area at an interface between air and water or solid surfaces and water. This affects such properties as the size of raindrops and the height to which water rises. It also influences cellular properties. Water among normal liquids exhibits a high value of surface tension.

The properties of water listed in *The Fitness of the Environment* are of importance in its biological and planetary role, and all represent extreme or nearly extreme values for water compared with all other possible substances. In Henderson's time, the reasons for the strange bulk-phase behavior could only have been guessed at, but in the intervening years we have come to understand many details of the molecular structure of solid, liquid, and gaseous water. It is now possible to present good physical chemical explanations of all the large-scale properties. This makes water less mysterious, although no less remakable.

Detailing observed properties of chemicals or cells in terms of the underlying atomic and molecular properties is a type of explanation known as reductionism. We can use this approach in exploring the behavior of water. It is a fine example of how scientists think, and a very satisfying case in point, because we can account for all of the properties so important to Henderson in terms of a very small number of molecular features. Understanding water can grab hold of one's interest in the same way that the ancient mariner took hold of Coleridge's narrator, and it is not going to let me go until the story is told.

Let's start the story by forming a mental image of a water molecule as it exists in vapor, far away from and uninfluenced by other molecules. The structure consists of an oxygen nucleus, two protons (hydrogen nuclei), and eight electrons. The three nuclei form a triangle, with a nucleus at each vertex and the two protons equidistant from the oxygen. The electrons cannot be precisely localized, but two electrons spend most of their time along the O-H line, closer on the average to the oxygen. Two other electrons tend to be found along the other O-H line. The remaining four electrons tend to cluster in pairs near the oxygen nucleus. The nuclei are not static but tend to vibrate and oscillate with respect to each other. The H-O-H angle is about 105°. This is all pretty standard stuff now and indeed doesn't vary very much from what Mrs. Thatcher very forcefully taught me in high school. Strange, though, she never mentioned Wolfgang Pauli.

The electrons in the oxygen-hydrogen bond spend more time near the oxygen nucleus than they do in the neighborhood of the hydrogen nucleus. As a result, there is a net positive electrical charge in the region of the hydrogen nuclei and a net negative electrical charge in the vicinity of the oxygens.

An equal positive and negative charge separated at some distance forms an object known as an electrical dipole. The dipole has been known ever since Ben Franklin and his colleagues established that there are two kinds of electrical charge. Much of the electrical interaction between molecules is now described in terms of forces between charges and dipoles or between dipoles and dipoles. Water molecules have two equal dipoles, one along each oxygen-hydrogen bond.

As I write down these descriptions of water molecules on a yellow pad spread out on my writing table, I realize that I am announcing them in a rather dogmatic way. It sounds as if these pronouncements had been handed down from Mount Sinai and I am transmitting them. That approach, as we have discussed, is not the way of science. The features of water being presented have been deduced from X-ray diffraction experiments, from dielectric dispersion experiments, and from spectroscopic measurement. An elaborate, consistent, and highly connected theory allows one to go from those experiments and others to the model of water now being discussed. Scientists have become so familiar with this approach that we talk in terms of the model without apologizing for the methodological flaws inherent in the way we use language. In any case mea culpa; all these dogmatic-sounding statements are simply abbreviated ways of rapidly getting at some features of modern science of major interest in order to arrive at a philosophical position. You and I are always invited to more detailed and more profound works. As a favorite author, former Lahaina Harbor rat Herman Melville, once wrote, "This whole book is but a draught—nay, but the draught of a draught, Oh, Time, Strength, Cash, and Patience!"

Next for the romance of two water molecules nearing each other. When they approach at the correct orientation, there is an electrical attraction between the positively charged hydrogen of one molecule and the negatively charged oxygen of the other (unlike charges attract).

This more or less stable attraction between water molecules is often referred to as the hydrogen bond. Electrical attractions of this nature are the primary determinants of the structure of ice and liquid water and explain the properties of those phases. The electrostatic interaction of energy between two nearby water molecules is about one-twentieth that of the strong "covalent" bond between oxygen and hydrogen within the molecule. The strong bonds determine the existence of individual water molecules (H_2O), while the weaker electrical bonds determine the nature of the interaction between molecules to form a liquid or solid.

All this talk about water is frankly making me thirsty, and I go for a can of diet soda in the ice chest. This is a dilute aqueous solution, and on reflection I think it must be one of the most expensive forms of water available. On the other hand, I venture that the ancient mariner would have been pleased to have had a supply aboard. In any case, off to less scientific matters, suggested by ice in the chest, which is rapidly melting as the sun beats down on the boat and makes my office uncomfortably hot. It's time for a swim and some more direct interaction with water. Then we can return with a cooler perspective.

A few hours have passed and I'm now ready to resume thoughts of ice, which is a crystal whose three-dimensional structure results from a regular network of hydrogen bonds and covalent bonds. Each atom of oxygen in ice is strongly chemically bonded to two hydrogens and more weakly electrically attracted to two hydrogen atoms from neighboring molecules. The four bond directions are at the appropriate angles, so that a given oxygen atom sits at the center of a tetrahedron of neighboring oxygens. A tetrahedron is an interesting geometric structure of four points all equally distant from each other, so that any three of them form the vertices of an equilateral triangle. This structure is well known to those dockmates involved in a totally nonscientific quest for pyramid power. The open structure of ice accounts for its low density: some 10 percent less than that of water at its freezing point. In the liquid the molecules are not held so far apart and are freer to approach each other and become more tightly packed. As a result, ice floats and a column of water freezes from the top down. This feature is of major significance in glaciation, oceanography, and the structure of lakes and rivers. It is an interesting example of a bulk property of global importance that can now be understood in molecular terms. The low density of the solid is a rare feature, shared with few chemical compounds. Water, as illustrated, is an extreme case.

To realize the significance of the expansion on freezing, envision a planet in a world where ice is denser than water. The coldest liquid would continually sink to the bottom and there freeze. The ice when formed could not readily be melted because the warm water would stay on the top. Year after year ice would crystallize in the winter and persist through the summer. Bottom-dwelling life could not exist. The bodies of water would be mostly ice, covered by a thin layer of liquid. The character of our planet and its weather, ice ages and all, come from the open, low-density structure of crystalline water.

The details of the weak electrical hydrogen bonds have been well studied because this type of interaction also helps determine the shape of nucleic acids and proteins, and is involved in cellular-energy transformation. A proton in a hydrogen bond is strongly attached to one oxygen by a covalent bond and weakly attached to another by an electrical charge. It is located between the two of them nearer to the bonded oxygen. The distances vary somewhat, but the general features appear to be quite universal. The proton is in an equilibrium position tied down by a covalent bond on one side and pulled by an electrostatic attraction on the other. On rare occasions it gets confused and hops out of its position and covalently associates with the neighboring oxygen.

Next consider a melting piece of ice in my ice chest. As heat is supplied, the energy goes into breaking hydrogen bonds. When about 15 percent of the bonds are broken, the crystal can't hold its shape and breaks down into very tiny microcrystalline domains, which can both pack more tightly and move around more freely than the uniform, open structure of pure ice. The microcrystals repeatedly form, break, and move around. All rearrangements result in normal water becoming fluid at 0° C and remaining liquid until 100° C. Below zero, 0° C, H_2O is a crystal and above 100° C it vaporizes into the individual molecules of gas. This temperature for phase change depends on the pressure.

The heat of melting ice is the energy required to break up 15 percent of hydrogen bonds and disorder the crystal. The subsequent collapse of the structure into a denser state explains the volume decrease on melting. The transition from ice to water is called a phase change. This latent heat of melting of water is also high when compared with other substances. The fact that a large amount of heat must be removed to freeze water protects plants and cold-blooded animals against frostbite, the tissue damage of freezing. The high latent heat also stabilizes the temperature of marine and coastal environments.

As the temperature of water is raised from the freezing point, conflicting tendencies come into effect. The more broken up the crystalline structure becomes, the more tightly the molecules pack (consider a trash compactor by way of analogy; the broken-up pieces fit into a smaller volume), but the faster the molecules move, the farther apart they tend to remain. These two factors result in water getting denser from zero to 4° C and then getting less and less dense at higher and higher temperatures, when the second effect takes over. The 4° C point marks the maximum density and naturally enough is the temperature to deep oceanic water. This constant-temperature deep-sea layer stabilizes many aspects of oceanic processes.

As energy is supplied to liquid-phase water, it is used in two ways. The increase of temperature means an increase in the speed and kinetic energy of the atoms and molecules. In addition, there is a continual disordering of the remaining microcrystals, which implies a supply of energy to break more hydrogen bonds. The amount of energy that must be supplied to raise the temperature of one gram by 1° C is called the specific heat. Owing to the number and strength of the hydrogen bonds, water has one of the highest specific heats of any ordinary substance. Only liquid ammonia is higher.

Since living organisms are made up mostly of water, the high heat capacity protects them against rapid temperature changes in the surroundings. Environments containing large bodies of water are also stabilized for the same reason. The very large day-night temperature changes in the desert are indicative of the fluctuations that might exist on a dry planet while day-night changes on the seashore are much smaller.

The heat capacity of ice is appreciably less than that of water because no hydrogen bonds must be broken in raising the temperature of the crystalline material, and energy needs to be supplied only to be distributed among the vibrations of the atoms in the crystalline solid.

A second phase change occurs when water goes from the liquid to the gas phase. At temperatures below the boiling point and relative humidities below saturation, this is normal evaporation. The energy required to evaporate one gram of water is called the heat of vaporization. Water shows an extremely high value of this parameter, which is why evaporation is so effective in getting rid of heat and maintaining temperature. This has been discussed as sweating, but a related phenomenon in plants involving water taken up by the roots and evaporated by the leaves is an ecological and meteorological process of major importance. Both organisms and environment are cooled by evaporation, providing another example of the fitness of a watery world.

The reason for the high heat of vaporization of water is the necessity of breaking four hydrogen bonds in order to remove a molecule of water from the bulk phase and transport it into the gas phase. Once again, it is the hydrogen bonds and the excellent fit that provide an electrostatic stickiness between molecules and impart to water its special properties. The more that is learned, the firmer is the conviction that water is truly a unique substance. One by one the bulk properties yield to a detailed molecular explanation.

To focus on just how special a material is, we can compare it with the similar-looking molecule hydrogen sulfide, H_2S, a compound best known from its smell, like that of rotten eggs. The gas-phase molecules have similar structures, but sulfur, being appreciably less electronegative than oxygen, carries a much smaller negative charge, resulting in a smaller dipole moment for the hydrogen-sulfur bond when compared with the hydrogen-oxygen bond. When this is transferred into bulk properties, hydrogen sulfide has a lower boiling point, freezing point, and heat of vaporization.

	H_2O	H_2S
Boiling Point	100° C	−61.80° C
Melting Point	0° C	−82.9° C
Heat of Vaporization	540 cal/gm	131.9 cal/gm

Comparing the heats of vaporization shows that the forces holding hydrogen sulfide together are only about one-fourth as energetic as those holding water together. As a result the H_2S melts and boils at much lower temperatures. All of the properties of water we have discussed thus far are a consequence of the strong intramolecular forces between neighboring molecules.

Most of the other properties of water arise from the electrical properties of both the individual molecules and the substance in bulk. All molecules are, of course, made up of heavy positively charged nuclei and much lighter electrons surrounding the nuclei. The total negative electrical charge of the electrons is equal to the total positive electrical charge of the nuclei. The electrons are very fast-moving, or in terms of quantum mechanics they are spread out in a probability cloud around the nuclei. If this distribution is symmetrical, the molecule has a very small dipole moment and is said to be nonpolar. Most organic solvents are of this type. An example of a very symmetrical molecule is methane, CH_4. The carbon nucleus is at the center of a tetrahedron, and the hydrogen nuclei are at the four vertices. The electrons are evenly distributed between the carbon and hydrogen nuclei.

Water molecules have, in contrast to methane, a quite asymmetric distribution of electrical charges. The outer-shell electrons tend to cluster close to the oxygen, leaving it with a net negative charge, while the protons, or hydrogen nuclei, having a deficit of electrons, show a net positive charge, resulting in substantial charge asymmetry. We have discussed this when talking about the dipole moment. Molecules with this kind of charge distribution are called polar, and they strongly interact with one another, with the positive parts of one molecule attracting the negative parts of neighboring molecules. Nonpolar molecules give rise to oil and waxy materials, while polar molecules tend to dissolve in water.

The polarity of molecules is measured by the dielectric constant. Water has one of the highest dielectric constants of common materials, and methane, as might be expected, has one of the lowest. The high dielectric constant, high solvent power, and high ionizing power of water are thus all related electrical properties, which depend on the asymmetric distribution of electric charge on the molecules. High surface tension results from the fact that the air at an air-water interface is nonpolar and water molecules have a lower energy inside the liquid than they do when spread out at the interface.

We can now account for all of the extreme properties of water noted by Henderson, and we can explain them in terms of basic physics, the structure of matter in terms of electrons and nuclei. Water is unique, but not mysterious. Its properties result from the laws out of which the universe is structured. As a consequence, water plays its extraordinary role in all four of the goespheres.

Let us return to a consideration of polarity of molecules and some interesting consequences. Reviewing what we have said, highly polar liquids are good solvents for ions and other polar molecules, while very nonpolar liquids are good solvents for nonpolar molecules, usually organic compounds of an oily nature. Substances that are polar and nonpolar usually form separate phases. In much less technical jargon, this is usually summed up as "oil and water don't mix."

This principle of phase separation based on polarity is crucial to the structure and function of biological membranes, which are very thin nonpolar layers separating the watery interior of the cell from its aqueous surroundings. Membrane formation requires the highly polar properties of water, thus giving another example of a detailed biological feature dependent on an extreme feature of water. In addition to polar and nonpolar molecules there is a third group: those that have a polar end and a nonpolar end within a single structure. They are called amphiphiles, meaning they "love both kinds" of solvents. The phrase "love both kinds" has a different meaning on the dock and in certain local bars, but we had better not get sidetracked by that issue. Amphiphiles are a fascinating class of molecules and are the basis of colloids and a whole group of interesting molecular structures. They are responsible for the existence of mayonnaise, and acount for the cleaning power of soap and the calming effect of "oil" on troubled waters. They also are the molecules that are the building blocks of biological membranes.

Among the amphiphiles are the polar lipids, molecules with a long, nonpolar oily portion attached onto a polar chemical group with a strong attachment to water. Given a collection of these molecules, the oily ends come together to form a two-layered structure in which all the nonpolar groups interact with each other and all the polar groups are in water. Such a structure grows in two dimensions and forms a plane. All biological membranes consist of bimolecular sheets formed in the way we have just described from amphiphilic molecules. The sheets seal the loose ends, resulting in closed shells, or vesicles. The forces that hold membranes together depend on the difference between the polar and the nonpolar oily ends of the amphiphiles. This universal principle of construction used in biological systems is inherent in a universe made of nuclei and electrons. That thought will recur when we get around to the biosphere.

Some additional features of water are seen in special biological roles. An example is the tensile strength. Normally, one thinks of this property in terms of a wire or metal bar. The tensile strength is the force per unit area that must be applied to break or abruptly deform the material by pulling on it. A column of water in a capillary tube possesses internal coherence due to the hydrogen bonds and as a result exhibits a high tensile strength. Consequently, a very high column of liquid may be maintained without breaking under gravity. This enables water from the roots to reach the top leaves of the tallest trees. The maximum possible height of trees is determined by the molecular inter-actions that resulted in the surface tension and tensile properties of water. The height is also determined by the earth's gravitational force, a global parameter deter-mined by the size and density of the planet. The exist-ence of giant sequoias represents another balance between molecular and global properties.

The past few years have witnessed the developing study of a newly understood property of water that appears to be almost unique to that substance, is a key element in biological-energy transfer, and was almost certainly of importance in the origin of life. The more we learn the more impressed some of us become with nature's fitness in a very precise sense.

By way of background consider the way in which electrical current is carried in various materials. The best-known conductors are metals that utilize the mo-tion of electrons in conduction bands. This is the mode of operation of the wires I use to repair the boat's electrical system. In polar liquids, on the other hand, the flow of current is almost entirely by the migration of positive and negative ions in solution. Consider ordinary salt, sodium chloride, in water. The salt crystal dissolves and enters the fluid as sodium and chloride ions. Each ion interacts with the surrounding water dipoles and becomes surrounded with a group of molecules called a hydration shell. When an electric field is applied to such a salt solution, sodium ions move toward the negative electrode and chloride ions flow toward the positive electrode. The result of the two charge flows is an electrical current through the solution.

In the mid-1900s it was discovered that electrical conductance in ice was due to protons hopping from one hydrogen bond to another in the crystalline array. Other substances were then found whose electrical properties depended on proton conductance; but again ice and water crystals appear to be extreme cases.

The proton conductance along hydrogen bonds, first seen in ice, was being explained at about the same time that transport of protons across the membrane was being discovered as a major step in energy transformation in cell organelles such as mitochondria, and chloroplasts. It now appears that biological systems use a similar method of proton transport as that discovered for ice. An entire world of protochemistry is being discovered in living systems that depends on the free migration of hydrogen nuclei.

Proton conductance has become a subject of central interest in biochemistry because of its role in photosynthesis and oxidative phosphorylation. These major biological energy sources utilize proton conductance and the existence of hydrated protons as ions, both major features of water. Once again fitness enters in, in the detailed way in which the molecular properties of water are matched to the molecular mechanisms of bio-energetics. A property never imagined in Henderson's time turns out to be a significant part of the fitness of the environment.

It is difficult continually to wax poetic about anything so commonplace as water. Yet every time scientists take a detailed look at this substance, they come away with the appreciation that it is as unusual as it is plentiful. Both of these attributes go into making the earth fit to be a living planet, and it is possible that water may be required to make any planet habitable.

CHAPTER 10

Hot and Cold Air

I am having great difficulty writing today. It is not that my muse has left—I can sense her sitting on the aft of the boom urging me on. What is causing the trouble is a very painful ring finger on my left, or writing, hand. A couple of days ago, after sailing around Molokai, we were motoring back into the wind at night when the jib, which we thought was tied down, let go. The eighteen or so square yards of material whipping around in a 20-knot blow proved quite formidable, and before we got it under control I had managed to crack a small bone in my finger joint. I didn't actually feel the pain until fifteen minutes after we got the sail under control, but that's another story dealing with mind and body.

At the very least my aching joint is a constant reminder that it's time to think about air, that invisible but powerful geosphere that also forms a vital part of our planet's existence and interacts strongly with a loose jib. On a calm day the atmosphere looks structure-less, but with nothing more than the instruments aboard (a thermometer, barometer, and wind-velocity meter), one would find considerable structure both along the surface and rising in altitude.

The horizontal structure, which includes the winds and large-scale movements of air masses, is caused prin-cipally by the unequal solar heating at different lati-tudes, resulting in an equatorial-to-polar heat flow, and by the forces exerted on a fluid surface by a rapidly rotating planet. The latter are called Coriolis forces and are responsible for the trade winds that were banging around the jib a few days back. These air movements are the basis of weather, which in the long term becomes climate. The east-to-west trade winds influence the pres-ent climate, and the westerlies, in the middle latitudes, will bring me my share of snow the next winter I spend in New Haven. While meteorologists understand the basic physics behind the weather, the surface of the planet—with its land and water masses, islands and mountains, forests and plains—is so complicated that prediction, as everyone knows, is very difficult. I recall once being caught in a hailstorm on Long Island Sound listening to a weather report from a station ten miles away telling me about the low chance of precipitation. Well, I am sure we all have our favorite weather stories, but they all attest to the complexity in the local struc-ture of the atmosphere.

Another type of atmospheric structure is seen as we rise in altitude. This is caused in part by the opposing forces of gravity and diffusion. It is also caused by a photochemical interaction of the atmosphere with the incoming solar radiation. This radiation promotes chemical reactions leading to interaction between the chemical and physical properties of the gaseous envelope that surrounds the earth.

Before we consider the structure of the atmosphere, there is the question of why a planet has an atmosphere at all. In the early days, when the earth presumably condensed out of interstellar debris, there may have been a hydrogen atmosphere, some of which was blown away by solar wind, a stream of charged particles emitted by the sun. As the planet aged and condensed further, there was an outgassing and molecules were cooked up from the interior much like the volcanic gases of today, which still add to our atmosphere and hydrosphere. In this location, one hundred or so miles away from the rumbling Kilauea, it is hard not to think of volcanic examples.

Once molecules surround the planet in the gas phase, gravity draws them down toward the surface, and diffusion driven by thermal kinetic energy tends to send them off into space. It is the balance of these two conflicting motions that results in an atmosphere. The force of gravity depends on the size and the density of a planet. The rate of diffusion mainly depends on the atmosphere's temperature.

The temperature of gases, as we have already discussed, is related to the speed at which molecules are moving about. More precisely, it is proportional to the average kinetic energy of motion, which numerically depends on the product of the molecular mass times the velocity multiplied by itself. Thus lighter-weight molecules move more rapidly than heavier ones.

Near the surface of the planet, where the pressure is high, molecules frequently collide with one another, exchanging energy and altering their speed and direction. At higher altitudes there are fewer collisions. At the edge of the atmosphere a molecule, which has acquired high velocity, starts to sail off into space. Gravity acts on it, but provided it is moving faster than a certain critical escape velocity, its speed overcomes gravity and the molecule leaves, never to return. At the highest altitudes the light-weight hydrogen and helium sometimes gain enough speed to escape. The heavier molecules almost never escape. Thus during the long history of the earth appreciable hydrogen and helium have been lost.

Jupiter is a very large planet that is cold because it is so distant from the sun. It is surrounded by a very dense hydrogen layer, which cannot escape and might properly be regarded as a hydrogen ocean rather than an atmosphere. Mercury is a small, very hot planet, totally lacking an atmosphere. Any gas-phase molecules that may have been present have escaped from the surface off into space.

The existence of an atmosphere is, therefore, the result of a subtle dynamic balance between two conflicting tendencies. Atmospheres can persist only for planets that have a certain range of values of radius, density, and temperature. The conditions for a gaseous sphere are not exceedingly exacting, but they are not all that common, either. Since it is difficult, if not impossible, to imagine planetary life without an atmosphere, we may regard earth's astrophysical parameters as being very fit for the existence of life.

The combined effects of gravity and diffusion result in the air's being densest at sea level and gradually decreasing with altitude. This change is governed by a barometric law, which allows us to calculate that on the surface of the earth the density decreases by a factor of 2 every 3.6 miles. Thus at the mile-high city of Denver the atmosphere is about 82 percent as dense as at the seacoast. At the top of Mount McKinley the atmosphere is 53 percent of its sea level value. At thirty-six thousand feet, where the big jets fly, the atmosphere is down to about one-third its sea level value. The barometric law is not exact because of other factors, but it describes how the atmosphere gradually thins out until it is no more. At two hundred miles up, the density is down to about 500 molecules per cubic centimeter. This is the exosphere, the region from which hydrogen and helium are escaping into outer space.

While the pressure drops continuously, the temperature profile of the atmosphere is more complex and defines a series of spherical shells surrounding the earth in onion-skin fashion. The division between the layers is not always sharp.

The lowest and of course best-known layer is the troposphere, which contains three-fourths of the mass of the atmosphere. It is characterized by a temperature drop of about 10° C for every mile rise in altitude, finally reaching −55° C at seven miles up. It is near the top of the troposphere where long-distance air travel takes place.

Above the troposphere lies the stratosphere, which has a constant temperature ($-55°$ C) for the first five miles and then begins to heat up gradually until it reaches $0°$ C at thirty miles up. This temperature marks the upper limit of the stratosphere, where pressure is about one-thousandth the value at sea level. The atmospheric layers from the Northern and Southern Hemispheres do not mix much with each other, resulting in much cleaner air in the industrially poorer southern half of the globe.

The next layer, the mesosphere, is about twenty miles in thickness and cools with height to $-90°$ C at its outer limit. The next and outermost layer, the thermosphere, heats up and thins out as it gets farther from the earth's surface. At one hundred fifty miles up the temperature is $300°$ C.

The atmosphere is structured in another way that we have not yet discussed: the chemical composition also varies as we rise from sea level to the thermosphere. Near the solid earth the composition is influenced by biological activity and the exchange of gases between the atmosphere and the ocean. As we rise there are ever-increasing chemical changes due to interaction between the most energetic components of the sun's radiation and the most photochemically active of the gas components.

Near the earth the composition of the dry atmosphere has been experimentally shown to be as follows:

	%
Nitrogen	78.084
Oxygen	20.964
Argon	.934
Carbon dioxide	.031
Neon	.00184
Helium	.00052
Methane	.00015
Krypton	.00011
Hydrogen	.00005
Nitrous oxide	.00003

The water content is variable and fluctuates between 0 and 1 percent.

It is well to consider how many of these molecules are related to biological processes. Nitrogen is fixed by conversion to ammonia by a group of soil and root module bacteria. Oxygen is produced by photosynthesis and consumed by respiration. Carbon dioxide is conversely used in photosynthesis and released in respiration. Methane is produced by certain bacteria in marshes, bogs, and wetlands. Nitrous oxide is produced by soil bacteria, and water enters into most biochemical pathways. In a certain very real sense the atmosphere is the gas phase of the biosphere, with a constant flow of molecules between the two compartments.

The carbon dioxide in the atmosphere also interacts with the ocean by dissolving in water and becoming converted to the bicarbonate ion, which may be used by algae or converted into insoluble carbonates. Tectonic processes may bring precipitated carbon to the surface again. As CO_2 values rise in the atmosphere, most of the increase is taken up by the oceans. Falling atmospheric CO_2 results in release by the ocean, thus tending to regulate atmospheric levels.

The relation of the atmosphere to the biosphere and other geospheres was discussed by J. E. Lovelock in his *Gaia* hypothesis. His ideas, in the tradition of Henderson's, present the results of a scientist's musing on the extraordinary fitness of the environment. Lovelock answers that the environment is fit because it is controlled by the biosphere in a self-regulating fashion.

The chemical composition of the atmosphere most influences the environment by affecting the temperature; the principal mechanism is the greenhouse effect. Focus for a moment on how a greenhouse works. Sunlight, with most of its energy in the visible range, passes through the glass windows into the greenhouse. After all, we have developed a glass industry because of the ability of that substance to transmit visible light. In the greenhouse most of the light is absorbed by the soil, the tile, the pots, and other nonliving components and is converted into heat. This process raises the temperature of the absorbers, which then radiate infrared. Glass absorbs rather than transmits infrared and thus heats up. An appreciable portion of the incident light energy stays in the greenhouse as heat. The phenomenon is not limited to greenhouses; it explains why in the bright sunlight the interiors of closed cars get so hot and uncomfortable to sit in.

The earth's atmosphere acts somewhat like a glass window in a greenhouse. It freely transmits visible light, which at the surface of the planet is largely converted to heat. Certain minor atmospheric components such as water vapor, carbon dioxide, and methane are good absorbers of infrared and therefore block the ready release of heat radiation to outer space. As a result, the surface of the planet is hotter than would be expected by a consideration of radiation balance alone, without the "greenhouse." Because the infrared-absorbing gases are in the atmosphere in low concentration, control of these gases by biological processes can profoundly influence the planet's temperature. Thus a minor component like the biosphere can have a very major effect on the planet's temperature and climate. This fact is at the core of Lovelock's Gaia hypothesis.

The radiation that leaves the sun and arrives at the earth is approximately that given off by a body of $5,875°$ K. At the very long (radio wave) and very short (X ray) wavelength ends of the spectrum there are higher intensities than would be expected, and this is understood in terms of solar physics. This radiation passes successively through the layers of the atmosphere, causing different photochemical effects at each level. The energetic photons are most reactive and are removed from the radiation as it travels downward. The most photoactive material is oxygen, which reacts and yields very active oxygen atoms (O) and ozone molecules (O_3). Atoms of oxygen occur at maximum concentration at an altitude of one hundred kilometers and ozone at about twenty-five kilometers. Ozone is itself a strong absorber of ultraviolet light so that very little radiation of wavelengths under 3,000 angstroms (near ultraviolet) falls on the earth's surface. Terrestrial life is protected from the destructive effects of intensive ultraviolet radiation.

The chemistry of the atmosphere is governed by the near-surface and hydrospheric production and consumption of gas-phase chemicals and the upper atmosphere reactions that produce and consume gaseous species. Consider methane as an example. It is produced in marsh gases and through the digestion of ruminants. At one point, farting cows were thought to be the world's chief source of methane, but further experimental evidence has dispelled that romantic notion. It is hard at first sight to believe that gas-producing ruminants are part of our global atmospheric chemical balance, but all components are interrelated. More than a billion tons of methane finds its way into the atmosphere by these processes every year. Most of it recombines with oxygen by a slow burning that helps to control oxygen levels. Some of it is diffused into the stratosphere, where reactions with oxygen continue giving rise to carbon dioxide and water. Some of the water photodissociates to oxygen, which stays in the earth's atmosphere, and to small amounts of hydrogen, which escape.

Another gas made in substantial amounts in the soils and seas is ammonia. While large quantities are produced, there are only traces in the atmosphere because it is rapidly used up neutralizing acid molecules that would otherwise cause naturally occurring acid rains. Nitrous oxide is another trace component of the atmosphere that is produced in the soil and sea and plays an important part in regulating the oxygen content of its air.

Surveying all these components of the atmosphere, Lovelock argues that they are regulated by the biosphere in order to somehow control its own environment. He maintains that the physical state of the planet is not a given set of conditions in which life must survive, but that the biosphere regulates the atmosphere and determines the climate and environmental milieu. If the environment is uniquely fit for life as Henderson maintains, Lovelock would argue that life works on the environment to make it uniquely fit.

The idea is a rather surprising one at first glance. We have up until very recently thought of the geological and meteorological states of the planet as being determined by astrophysical and geophysical factors. In the course of studying these factors and investigating the processes that take place, we find that the biosphere, largely through its effect on the atmosphere, exerts extensive control on global planetary factors. We may draw an analogy. Just as beavers building dams, corals building reefs, and humans constructing condominiums create a local environment to survive, so does all of life construct a global shield of gas to regulate the temperature, water composition, and chemical balance so as to create a habitable and comfortable planet. We and our environment are one.

When Jesus of Nazareth delivered the Sermon on the Mount and when Gautama Buddha elaborated on the eightfold way, each breathed out about 120 quarts of air. Since the molecules they exhaled have become uniformly distributed in the earth's atmosphere during the course of the ages, every breath we inhale includes about 250 molecules from each of those two great discourses. All life on the surface of the earth is interrelated because we share the same atmosphere, the same oceans, the same natural resources; in short, because we share the same planet. The interrelatedness of living things has long been discussed by philosophers and theologians. It is now clear from science alone that the interrelatedness is built into the laws of nature in the most fundamental ways. For this planet, life processes are part of the regulatory mechanisms that maintain all of nature in a self-sustaining manner. If that isn't design, I don't know what is.

CHAPTER 11

Water, Water, Everywhere

Since walking on lava provided such a good setting for thinking about the lithosphere, I've decided that a day at sea should provide the inspiration for writing about the hydrosphere. Some folks around here would say we're just looking for an excuse to take a day off and go sailing, but we'll ignore these mean-spirited jibes.

So with Lucille at the tiller, two friends in the cockpit, and me at the table below with a book called *Oceans, Second Edition*, we are off in the direction of Kahoolawe. It is an overcast day and the winds are light and seem to be shifting from northwesterly trades to southerly konas. The seas are quite calm and things look quieter than usual. Indeed, it is noticeably quiet, almost eerie, out on the waters.

About two miles offshore, there is a shout of "Look

over there," and I hurry up to the cockpit to see what's going on. About half a mile away are a group of humpback whales. We fall off, change direction, and slowly move toward the spouting animals. We have done this many times before, always drawn by the possibility of a closer look at these huge animals. They usually respond by sounding and swimming away. It's a sort of game sailors and whales play during the Hawaiian winter.

As we get closer, we see that the group of animals consists of four adults and one calf. Quite unlike their behavior at our previous sightings, the whales do not swim away but hold their territory and circle around the boat. For the next ten of the most exciting minutes any of us has ever experienced, the humpbacks remain very close. They are so near we can hear them breathe, smell them, and feel the spray. One of our friends is up on the foredeck in a rush of picture taking. And then the whales decide they have had enough communicating; they have satisfied their curiosity and swim off.

When it was certain they would return no more, I went back to my writing desk below and set down the following lines:

Come you baleened behemoths
You large-brained biota
Share what's on your minds
You have spent several million years
Swimming round with few enemies
Until a killer species appeared

You had sufficient time to think
To compose symphonies, to meditate
About the creator of cetacean kind.
We once had a philosopher named Thales
Who believed that all things are water
Whales, Do you read me?

Look, you long-lived leviathans,
You fabulous fluked fauna
Let us in on your knowledge
We were so occupied with our prehensile thumbs
And converting our monkey brains to metaphysics
We never had the time nor concentration
That you were able to devote to pure thought.
We once had a philosopher named Einstein
Who maintained all things are relative to the observer
Titans, Do you hear me?

Consider it, you gigantic geniuses
You marvelous monumental mammals
Won't you part with a few clues
A small sample of your vast lore
We were learning to fashion harpoons
And thus had little inclination for ethics
But you floating around and frolicking
Had much leisure for such things.
We once had a philosopher named Melville
Who hinted that you fathomed the secrets of the universe
But his name I only whisper to you, whales.

And if we shared the cetacean experiences of the ocean, we should be way ahead in our knowledge of the hydrosphere. For the great whales migrate from the polar circles to the tropics, and some species even move between the great oceans. Although they surface to breathe, they can sound to considerable depths, and hence they probably experience more of the hydrosphere than any other group of animals.

Like the atmosphere the oceans show variability both vertically and horizontally. Important factors are temperature, salinity, oxygen content, and chemical composition. Strong ocean currents maintain a global pattern of circulation, and nutrient upwelling determine areas of high biological productivity. The major oceans, the Atlantic, Pacific, and Indian, connect with each other through the Southern Ocean, and the Atlantic and Pacific connect through the Arctic Ocean.

In a certain sense, the oceans act like "a gigantic pump that transfers heat from the equator to the poles." This is a process we also note in the atmosphere. More solar energy arrives in equatorial regions, rendering them the hottest parts of the planet, and heat flows from hot to cold regions.

Many forces are operative in creating ocean currents. Several of these depend on density differences of water. Above 4° C the density of water decreases with increasing temperature and increases with salinity.

Under the influence of solar radiation, water evaporates from the ocean surfaces and precipitates in a global pattern of rain and snow. The water falls back on the oceans or the land, where it eventually returns to the ocean, carrying dissolved minerals and particulate materials in the swiftly flowing rivers. The hydrological cycle provides a strong link between water, air, and earth.

The major flows of water in the oceans are wind-driven on the surface and gravity-driven by differences of density in the subsurface waters. The surface flows in different parts of the world have names such as the Gulf Stream, the Brazil Current, the Kuroshio, and the Peru Current. Below the polar-directed surface flows there are deep equatorial return flows.

All of the major currents are governed by budgets for heat, water, and salt. Globally, there must be an approximate balance between heat in and heat out, water in and water out, salt concentration and salt dilution. All three of these budgets are related, since heat causes evaporation and concentration of salt. Because the organisms that live in the sea also depend on temperature and salinity, oceanic life depends on the various physical states.

The oceans are a reservoir for carbon dioxide, for there is constant exchange between atmospheric gases and dissolved bicarbonate ions. In addition, the dissolved material can interact with calcium to form calcium carbonate precipitates, which sink into the benthos. The hydrosphere thus participates in regulating the atmospheric levels of carbon dioxide, which in turn influence the weather by the greenhouse effect.

The atmosphere and hydrosphere are in constant dynamic interaction. This is most dramatically seen in phenomena like El Niño, the Child. The unlikely name was coined by Spanish-speaking South American fishermen who noticed the sudden warming of the waters along the eastern coast of Peru and Ecuador around Christmas. El Niño is a very massive shift in winds and currents over the entire Pacific Basin. It does not occur annually but irregularly in time and is particularly severe every few years. The most severe El Niño in recent times, 1982–83, resulted in droughts in Australia and in Southeast Asia, floods in South America, and the massive death of fish off Peru and Ecuador.

Normally the southern Pacific has east-to-west winds. In an El Niño this pattern partially reverses, shifting weather throughout the entire tropical ocean basin. There seems to be a vast oscillation in these conditions taking an irregular time period. While scientists do not fully understand El Niño, they are convinced it is part of an interactive cycle of hydrosphere and atmosphere, neither of which can be studied in isolation.

My modest attempts to understand the hydrosphere have convinced me that not only are the oceans vast and deep but the complexity of physical, chemical, and biological processes taking place is also vast and deep. I have pointed out how difficult it is to understand the details of weather and atmosphere, but it would seem the oceans are even more difficult. What is clear is that the great bodies of water are strongly interactive with each other, with the land, and with the atmosphere. No aspect of global process can be understood in isolation. And beyond the details lies the bottom line of my story. Every aspect of the earth is so highly interrelated that it is not meaningful to try to isolate organismic life without understanding it in a planetary context.

I'm still left with the feeling that the whales are far ahead of me in understanding the oceans. If we could only institute a little collaborative research, we might both come out with a better understanding of the world. I'm ready if they are.

CHAPTER 12

What Is Life?

Among the repertoire of tunes sung by the Whiffen-poofs of Yale is an entertaining number called "Too Darn Hot." With the approach of summer the cabin of the boat in the afternoon is getting just too darn hot for writing. The nearest shade is the huge banyan tree in the center of town, and that seems appropriate enough; after all, Buddha had spent time under a banyan tree before he came to his final tree of meditation. Of course he didn't have tourists to contend with, but I'm getting pretty experienced at shutting out the world around me while concentrating on global issues. And the time has come to focus on the fire of life and the search for its elusive secret.

Many a whimsical story has been told of the travels and travails of seekers who wander great distances, finally drop at the feet of long-sought-after gurus, and implore, "What is Life?"

In one such tale, the traveler comes to a renowned sage high up on the mountains of Nepal and pleads for the secret of life. The loincloth-adorned, very aged, wizened master peers at him with twinkling eyes and replies, "Buy when everyone else sells, sell when everyone else buys, and lead a rich sex life."

In another verson the searcher comes to the great Rebbe in Safed and pleads, "What is Life?" The sage answers, "Life is a fountain." The supplicant gets angry and says, "I've traveled halfway around the world, spent all my money, exhausted myself, and all you can tell me is that Life is a fountain?"

"All right, my son," says the Rebbe. "In that case, Life is not a fountain."

The very words "What is Life?" have a particularly nostalgic ring for me, for *What Is Life?* is the title of a book by physicist Erwin Schrödinger that was instrumental in my choice of biophysics as a career. Such memories run deep and I periodically reread this book as an example of Schrödinger's great wisdom and foresight. The current answers to the question set forth by Schrödinger follow in part from the way he formulated that question and the influence his book had on a generation of scientists.

It is hard to present a universal conception of the biosphere, the entire world of the living, because so many different people have held such diverse views of life. Putting aside for the moment the guru of Nepal and the Rebbe of Safed, even among biologists there has been a great diversity of views about the nature of life. Four of these seem to cover the central ideas and establish the perspective I'd like to focus on. First, there are those who would point to the two million or so extant species of organisms and the countless millions of extinct species and find life within the myriad forms that exhibit this strange property of being alive. Second, there are those who would peer through the great diversity and concentrate on the unity of cells, organelles, and common biochemical processes in order to seek the necessary and sufficient molecular hardware that underlies all the enigmatic manifestations of life. Third, there are those who would look at ecosystems, the necessary relations between living things, to see how organisms taken together in their environment have properties, unrealized when they are viewed as individuals. This view focuses on the role of life in nature and nature in life. A fourth group of scientists seeks defining relations to envision life deep within the laws of physics and the nature of the cosmos. There is a legitimacy to all of these approaches, for as in the tale of the blind men and the elephant each focuses on partial insights. When taken in their totality, these bring us nearer to our original question.

And so under the banyan tree in the park there is the leisure to explore one of the eternal queries. The first approach to the question "What is life?" is the least abstract, the viewing of actual organisms, and we turn to a modern version of the classification system first put forward by Carl von Linné, a perceptive Swedish botanist, in the early 1700s. Using a modern group of taxa undreamed of by the founder of taxonomy, all of life is now divided into two superkingdoms: procaryotes, or simple unicellular forms without complex intracellular organelles, and eucaryotes, which include everything else. The procaryotes encompass the bacteria and blue-green algae, the simplest microorganisms. The cells do not have nuclei or other conventional cell apparatus. The eucaryotes include the two traditional kingdoms of Linné, the plants and animals, and a third group, the protists, a varied collection of protozoa, algae, fungi, and other difficult-to-classify organisms. In the late 1980s it seems strange that the word "kingdom" is used for the major taxa. That clearly tells us more about Europe in 1735 than it does about biology, for it was a time when all the world was divided into kingdoms.

Of all possible methods of cell organization only two, the procaryotes and eucaryotes, have persisted. Cells are either very simple, like the bacteria, or highly complex, with the possibility of sexual replication, like everything else. There are no intermediate modes of organization. It is unusual that there are two and only two types of organizations, with no intermediate forms, and the reason for that result seems beyond us at the moment.

The world of living beings comes in a bewildering array of sizes, shapes, feeding patterns, and modes of survival. Organisms range in magnitude from the tiny mycoplasma, a few thousand atomic diameters across, to blue whales and giant sequoias whose mass is counted in tens and hundreds of tons. Fish live in the subfreezing cold of arctic waters and blue-green algae grow in the scalding temperature of hot springs and geysers. Reproductive strategies range from simple binary fission to the elaborate courtship and mating patterns of birds, fish, and mammals. In humans, sexuality and courtship have become central features of biological and social existence. I must note there has also been an opportunity to observe this activity on the Lahaina dock.

My own research has over the years involved some of this range of properties. I have studied tiny mycoplasma in the laboratory and have worked with humpback whales in the waters off Maui. I have investigated the survival of brine shrimp at $-271°$ C, just two degrees above absolute zero, and *Bacillus stereothermophilus* at $60°$ C. I have experimented with *E. coli*, which can live almost anywhere, and with species of mesozoans who can complete their life cycle only within the kidney of an octopus. And so the great variety of the living world has impressed itself upon me. I have known it visually and tactually as well as intellectually.

The world of living organisms is the biosphere, as encountered by Thoreau at Walden Pond. It encompasses the plants and animals that lived around and within the ponds, reproduced, grew, and filled the naturalist's surroundings with daily fascination. One recalls his description of war between two species of ants, the migration of birds, or the fish swimming in the pond. The world of nature as it presents itself to us provides one great, graphic, tangible answer to the query What is Life?

Behind the great diversity of millions of present and past species are common features shared by every living thing. All life is made of cells, tiny units surrounded by a thin oily membrane. All of life processes its energy through molecules of adenosine triphosphate. All life is made up of proteins, nucleic acids, fatty acids, and sugars. All life encodes its information in DNA and uses the same universal code. All cells use the same apparatus of protein synthesis, including ribosomes, and transfer and messenger RNAs. This catalog could go on and on in more and more detail, for the common features of molecular hardware are numerous and the rules have universal applicability.

Within these generalizations the molecular biologist seeks the essence of life. It is sought in those organelles and molecules that have such remarkable similarity in all living things. The approach is called reductionism. The function of organisms is explained in terms of cells and tissues. Cells are studied as collections of organelles, which are understood as collections of macromolecules. Large and small molecules are understood in terms of physics and chemistry. It is, of course, a retrospective study, since we are at present unable to infer the necessity of life from the properties of atoms and molecules.

This distinction between diversity and unity, between looking at the totality of life and seeking universal principles, is not new. For example, we find in the works of Aristotle in *De partibus animalium* the following:

> Ought we, for instance . . . to begin by discussing each separate species—man, lion, ox, and the like—taking each kind in hand independently of the rest, or ought we

rather to deal first with the attributes which they have in common in virtue of some common element of their nature, and proceed from this as a basis for the consideration of them separately?

The details have changed greatly and the knowledge has expanded enormously, but our first two views of life have a grand history.

The third view of life is the province of the general ecologist, who recognizes that all living things must take in energy and matter and process them into forms appropriate to growth and replication. This forces one to look at the initial input of energy into the entire ecosystem, its flow-through to various parts, and its ultimate exit. Similarly, the inflow and outflow of matter leads to consideration of the great global cycles of carbon, nitrogen, sulfur, and phosphorus. Such a view focuses on the relation between species, between the eater and the eaten.

Our understanding of the physical universe is in terms of matter, energy, and structure or information. All active processes are driven by the flow of energy. It is not accidental that global biology is powered in this way; it is an absolute necessity imposed by the basic laws of physics. In fact, any dynamic system will operate in a similar fashion.

At the base of every ecological system are the primary producers, organisms who take in energy from the environment. These organisms are also designated the first trophic level and are largely photosynthesizers—plants, bacteria, and algae that take in the sun's energy and convert it into a chemical form suitable for biochemical usage.

At the second trophic level are the grazers, organisms that get their energy by eating primary producers or their products. Cows, elephants, seed-eating birds, phytoplankton-eating zooplankton, fruit-eating monkeys, and countless other species acquire their energy by consuming plants and algae. The carbon that has been fixed by photosynthesis, the nitrogen that has been converted to ammonia by bacteria, and the sulfur and phosphorus from the soil flow along their cyclic pathways.

The grazers are eaten by carnivores, the carnivores by top carnivores, and ever present are the saprophytes ready to eat dead organisms, the excreta of organisms, and other products of rot and decay. Because the same energy and matter are flowing through all these levels, they are closely related in one vast complex, interconnected network. The study of life within this context becomes the study of the relationship between organisms, who eats whom and why.

A newly discovered ecosystem shows the generality of this approach. In the sunless depths of the seas in the deep Galápagos trench off the coast of South America, volcanic action bubbles up hydrogen sulfide. Certain bacteria are able to oxidize this sulfur compound and use the energy obtained to carry out all their necessary biological processes. These bacteria are the first trophic level for this system. They are eaten by tiny animals that are in turn eaten by larger animals and so on up the trophic chain, leading to a complete ecological system operating independently of the light of the sun yet fulfilling our general description of an energy-flow process. Chemical energy as hydrogen sulfide flows in and heat flows out, maintaining the biological integrity of the system.

A fourth view of life temporarily sets aside all the fascinating hardware of atoms, molecules, organelles, cells, organisms, and ecosystems in order to focus on the most general functional properties, the ultimate logic of life. To use a computer analogy, we are inquiring into the irreducible software, the mathematics necessary to program what we recognize as life within the constraints of the "hardware" rules. This will nevertheless have certain consequences in terms of the kinds of objects that are able to conform to the logic.

To elaborate on the hardware-software distinction, the former consists of the molecules of proteins, nucleic acids, and the like, which are common to all living forms. At a molecular level these are the working parts of living organisms as the silicon chips, switches, and wires are the working parts of a computer. The software of life, the programs and logic by which it functions, are, at present, not so well understood as the hardware, yet we need to probe it to know if life is unique to our type of planet, to carbon chemistry, to the presence of water, and to any other features that are peculiar to the earth. We are thinking about features that any entities would have to possess in order for us to recognize them as alive. This has been stated in its most cosmic form by biophysicist J. D. Bernal, who said, "A true biology in its full sense would be the study of the nature and activity

of all organized objects wherever they were to be found
—on this planet, on others in the solar system, in other
solar systems, in other galaxies—and at all times, future
and past." Our scope will not be as broad as his statement, but it is nice to have the ultimate quotation before
us.

Some of these more abstract approaches to the nature
of life went into choosing the experiments for the Viking
Lander to perform on Mars in order to look for life.
With only a minimal knowledge of the chemistry of the
unexplored surface, scientists wished to look for those
activities we would recognize as life. This approach
required a much more general view than one is usually
required to assume in dealing with earthly biology. The
results to date suggest the absence on Mars of what we
would clearly recognize as life, although interesting
chemical cycles appear to be taking place.

In inquiring about the nature of life, we will next
act somewhat like the enigmatic Zen masters and start
by talking about something that seems far removed from
the subject. We turn to the laws of thermodynamics.
Life appears to be a deep property of the cosmos, and
our probe of its nature must take us into the laws of
physics, which are among the most successful approaches mankind has devised to probe profound questions. Nobel laureate biochemist George Wald once
wrote that a physicist is the atom's way of understanding atoms. And in that spirit we proceed.

Living things, whatever else they may be, are made
up of atoms and molecules, the same basic building
blocks as the rest of the universe. Either living beings

obey the laws of physics or those laws lose the power of generality. It may be that the understanding of life or thought goes beyond our present-day physical science, but we find it difficult to imagine a systematic violation of those laws. Indeed, the approach is to start with the known and look beyond in our search for meaning. Starting with basics, one must include energy, entropy, temperature, and order to arrive at an abstract understanding of what we mean by life.

Lying behind our understanding of all biological phenomena are the first and second laws of thermodynamics. The first states that energy is conserved; if we are studying a system, the change in its energy is the amount that has been taken in minus the amount that has flowed out. Energy can neither be created nor destroyed in the system.

Energy is perhaps the most important concept of physics. Much of nineteenth-century research in that field was devoted to understanding energy and learning to measure it with precision in all its forms. It is still the central construct of natural philosophy that dominates theory in every branch from particle physics to biophysics. The theory of general relativity with the famous $E = mc^2$ equation allows, of course, for the conversion of mass into energy. If we include mass as one of the forms of energy, then the previous statement of the first law of thermodynamics holds for all systems.

Back when we were talking about propaedeutics I talked about how I would explain energy to my neighbors, and here I am at it again. But I'm not being repetitious; we're moving ahead to try to understand energy even more deeply. So whatever I used to lure my neighbors then, I would now repeat with the ultimate promise of the excitement of finding out how things really work.

Energy, then, may flow into a system as heat, radiation, or work done on the contents. It may also enter accompanying the entry of matter. For example, if gasoline and oxygen flow into an engine cylinder, there is an obvious influx of energy quickly demonstrated when ignition takes place. Energy may flow out of a system by the same set of processes.

Physicists recognize three types of systems with respect to the flow of matter and energy. *Isolated systems* have no flow of either kind. An example of such an entity would be the inside of a very well-insulated box. *Closed systems* have a flow of energy but no flow of matter. An example of such an object would be the inside of the same insulated box now equipped with a window through which light or heat may pass. The surface of the earth is also a good approximation of a closed system since the only flow of matter is an occasional meteorite in and hydrogen leaking out from the upper atmosphere. There is, however, a constant flow of electromagnetic energy in from the sun and out through infrared radiation to outer space. A third category consists of *open systems*, which let both energy and matter flow in and out.

With a knowledge of the different kinds of systems we can move to the second law of thermodynamics, which states that isolated systems tend toward the maximum degree of molecular disorder consistent with the total energy they possess. This molecular disorder is numerically measured by the amount of entropy, so the second law is often worded in terms of the entropy of isolated systems continually increasing until it reaches a maximum value when the systems come to equilibrium.

Organized systems also have a tendency to decay into disorder, but that tendency can be countered by taking in high-grade energy, using it to do work to order the system, and rejecting low-grade energy, usually as heat, into the surroundings. Isolated systems cannot remain ordered; the maintenance of states away from equilibrium requires the constant flow-through of energy. And so we have the most general property of the class of entities to which living things belong, the maintenance of order by the flow-through of energy.

Further examining the fourth view of life we can move on to a definition put forward many years ago by a microbiologist, J. Perrett. I believe that his statement forms a consensus that would be agreed to by most biologists. If it lacks the awesome generality of Bernal's cosmic view, it has the kind of precision that would serve a group of exobiologists seeking life on other planets and in other solar systems. Perrett noted: "Life is a potentially self-perpetuating open system of interlinked organic reactions, catalyzed stepwise and almost isothermally by complex and specific organic catalysts which are themselves produced by the system." This sounds like jargon, but it is really a very condensed way of saying a great deal about life, which can be understood phrase by phrase. The next few pages will explore the words and provide the background so that we can move on with a commonly held understanding of what we mean by life.

First, let us focus on the idea that life is an open system, or more precisely that living organisms are open systems. Life is a property, whereas living organisms are entities. The definition is in terms of open systems and therefore describes types of objects. These grammatical problems are not trivial, as we are heading toward describing life as a property of planets rather than of entities called living organisms. The above definition should begin "Life is a property of a potentially . . ."

We then return to the idea that living organisms are open systems. "System" is used in a thermodynamic sense. It is some volume or region of space that we can imagine to be surrounded by an imaginary surface. The concept allows us to distinguish, for analysis, a definite small volume from the rest of the universe.

If the imaginary surface does not correspond to an actual barrier, then the system is continuous with its surroundings and has no existence as an entity in the usual sense. Consider, then, actual separation mechanisms. There might be a complete barrier that would prevent the flow of any matter or energy across a membrane. That would lead to an isolated system. There might be a barrier to the flow of matter but not energy, resulting in a closed system. There might be a barrier that partially restricts the flow of matter and energy. An example of this would be a semipermeable membrane of the type used in osmosis experiments. It lets through little molecules and excludes big ones.

A totally isolated system cannot maintain life for extended periods of time. Consider a thought experiment with a balanced, sealed aquarium or terrarium in a rigid insulating box through which there is no flow of light or heat. The plants in the absence of light would cease to grow. The animals would run out of food and die, and the breakdown processes would eventually fill the box with carbon dioxide, ammonia, nitrogen, and other products of decay. The contents of the insulated box would heat up from the chemical reactions taking place. This would further speed the decay, and in a very long time the contents would completely degrade to a chemical equilibrium of the most thermodynamically stable molecules.

In a second thought experiment take the same kind of sealed aquarium or terrarium used in the previous experiment and place it in constant-temperature surroundings. Again, in the absence of light, photosynthesis would cease and the system would move toward a state of death, decay, and ultimately chemical equilibrium, or maximum entropy. If we introduce a light source and the system is properly balanced, it can maintain itself in a living state for a long period of time. Such sealed ecosystems have been developed by experimentalists and have persisted for several years. They are maintained by the flow of energy—light in, heat out.

The type of microecosystem we are describing is closed to the flow of matter and open to the flow of energy in the form of electromagnetic radiation. An individual organism must be open to the flow of matter as well as energy because at the very least it exchanges oxygen, carbon dioxide, and water with its surroundings. To grow, it must take in molecules in one form or another. Living organisms must be open systems. They have to obtain energy either as light or food and exchange matter as food, respiratory gases, or waste products.

In order to be an open system, any entity must be surrounded by a barrier. At the cellular level this barrier is a membrane, a very thin, oily layer of molecules that surrounds the cell and controls the flow of other molecules both in and out. In larger systems the barriers are more complicated, but they always are structured in one way or another of cellular membranes.

Returning to Perrett's definition, the open systems are required to be self-perpetuating; that is, to be alive is to persist, to counter entropic decay by constantly regenerating damaged parts and growing replacement cells. Self-perpetuation comes in two ways: by the repair of existing organisms or parts of organisms or by reproduction, the synthesis of new organisms with the same genetic message as the progenitors. Since all life on earth appears to be a continuous stream going back for more than three billion years, the idea of persistence is a crucial one.

The word "potentially" in "potentially self-perpetuating open system" reminds us that life can rest in the form of seeds or spores and can persist in this way for quite a while, since these stages of suspended animation have evolved for the very purpose of slowing down the degradative processes. Dry brine shrimp eggs may retain their ability to germinate for hundreds of years. Seeds taken from the pyramids of Egypt have sprouted after around two thousand years. In the end, however, even these systems must regenerate by growth or they, too, decay and die.

Next we come to a description of the system as "interlinked organic reactions." "Organic" implies the use of carbon chemistry. It is a limitation of life to the kinds of chemicals we are familiar with. The author could have been more general by saying "interlinked chemical reactions." Yet when scientists look at the periodic table of the elements, the array of all possible kinds of atoms, the uniqueness of carbon and nitrogen in terms of their ability to form large, stable compounds is so outstanding that we find it hard to envision life, even in Perrett's very general sense, with any other atomic building blocks. A number of very able chemists have looked at these issues and they all seem to be persuaded that the differences among atoms is great enough to impose some severe limits on which elements can be used for life. It is good to be cautious and not dogmatic in these matters, but carbon chemistry seems to be a necessary feature of the life process.

Next the reactions are described as "catalyzed stepwise and almost isothermally by complex and specific organic catalysts." If within a living cell all possible chemical reactions could take place, the results would be total chaos, a mixture of millions and millions of chemical compounds devoid of plan or meaning. Instead, what happens is that the only chemical reactions that occur at significant rates are those for which catalysts are present. The catalysts (enzymes, in the case of living cells) select out of all possible chemical reactions a small limited subgroup that will actually take place. The feature that characterizes living systems is that the specific catalysts are "themselves produced by the system." This guarantees the self-perpetuating features because the produced catalysts direct the system's chemistry to favor their own synthesis.

The idea of "stepwise and almost isothermal" catalysis assures a steady, orderly set of chemical reactions as contrasted to explosions or flames, which might be self-perpetuating but could not develop the kinds of large molecules demanded as specific catalysts. The implication is that a cell or organism has to be a chemical machine, not a heat engine.

The definition does not mention any specific hardware, but one could deduce from it the necessity of a boundary membrane, some kind of information storage mechanism, and an apparatus for the synthesis of specific catalysts.

We can now look at the interrelations among the four views of life. The abstract definition faces the question in the most general chemical-physical terms (with the exception of the word "organic") and provides a logical basis for seeking life anywhere in the universe. The molecular view of life provides a very detailed description of the one planetary case we know, a hardware embodiment of the logic of life. It may be a unique embodiment of the logic, or it may be one of many possible examples of the phenomenon. We are at the moment unable to decide among these two possibilities. What is known is the universality of the molecular hardware strategy among living creatures on the earth. All the millions of species share many features of the metabolic and genetic machinery. It is usually argued that the great similarities come from common descent, but there may be even deeper constraints. A relation between the logic and the hardware must clearly exist, but we have yet to fully understand it. We can look forward to wondrous new insights in this area when that relation is grasped.

If the principles of molecular biology are a chemical embodiment of the logic of life, then the range of living organisms encompasses the broader application of those principles of molecular biology. For each species represents a workable plan by which the mechanisms and components can be assembled into a functioning unit.

The allowable units are not, however, independent of each other or of their environment. Every parasite needs its host, every grazer needs its producers, and each predator needs its prey. Animals require the carbon fixation by plants, and both require nitrogen fixation by bacteria. Plants and animals require the gas exchange with the atmosphere, and as we have seen previously the atmosphere itself may be regarded as the gaseous part of the biosphere, for its chemical composition is heavily influenced by the activities of living organisms. The atmosphere interacts with the ocean by way of dissolved gases, and the atmosphere and hydrosphere interact by way of the hydrological cycle.

Thus the ecological view of biology stresses the interaction of organisms with one another and with the environment. But the environment is not an abstract given geophysical entity. It is strongly influenced by the metabolic activity, growth, and eroding effects of organisms, and the atmosphere is largely composed of biospheric gases. Each of the original three geospheres—earth, air, and water—is profoundly influenced or, as Lovelock suggests, regulated by the activities of organisms.

Beginning with the question "What is Life?" we focus on general properties of living organisms and discover the difficulties of considering a given being in isolation. When John Donne wrote "No man is an island, entire of itself," his intent was clearly psychological, but in a physical-chemical sense no living thing is an island unto itself, but each must be considered relative to its physical and biological environment.

Actually Donne's statement in its entirety does encompass aspects of the material sense in which we are all interrelated. He wrote:

> No man is an island, entire of itself; every man is a piece of the Continent, a part of the main. If a clod be washed away by the sea, Europe is the less, as well as if a promontory were, as well as if a manor of thy friends or of thine own were. Any man's death diminishes me, because I am involved in mankind. And therefore never send to know for whom the bell tolls; it tolls for thee.

Thus, for example, tales of the Loch Ness monster do not have a ring of credibility. A monster would require a population of similar creatures that would affect the food chain of the entire lake. A monster would require ancestors that would have deposited fossils or more recent remains. A monster would produce excreta that would take its place in the Loch Ness ecology. An isolated organism living apart from its biological setting is implausible. For observations to become science, they require credibility, a connectivity to a theoretical structure we have confidence in. The theory of the Loch Ness monster is totally devoid of such connectivity.

The physical and biological environments are inseparable; they interact with and regulate each other. Thus life is a collective property of all the interacting entities. In a very real sense, life is a planetary property whose very local manifestations are individual organisms. Those local manifestations embody exquisite molecular detail. A view of the biosphere must relate the molecular features to the global features. To fully understand life we must be able to reconcile ecological and molecular perspectives.

At the risk of being repetitious, it's worth mulling over this idea that life is a planetary property. In a controlled, isolated laboratory situation an organism can exist and can remain alive in a regulated environment where food and oxygen are brought in and waste is eliminated. In nature a species avoids extinction by obtaining energy and nutrients from an environment that must be maintained within acceptable limits with respect to temperature, pH, presence of toxic substances, supply of trace minerals, and a number of other requirements. These limits are maintained by the cycling processes of the atmosphere, hydrosphere, and lithosphere and by regulatory feedbacks among the four geospheres with particular effects of the biosphere on the atmosphere and hydrosphere. All of these components must work together, and everything must be right in order for a planet to maintain life.

CHAPTER 13

History of the Universe

Haleakala is a large red-black-and-gray volcanic mountain with a crater at the top large enough to fit Manhattan Island. The hike through the crater, in from Sliding Sands and out through the switchback at Halemau'u, takes about six hours. It's a walk I take because the air is clear, and the multicolored, rugged scenery is quiet and soothing. My fellow hiker is a botanist with an impressive knowledge of local flora, so it's a learning experience as well as a hike. Actually, I'm working myself up to tell the story of the history of the universe from the "big bang" until the present, and these gray cinder cones and red laval hills set the tone. I have on other occasions slept out here under the stars, and that, too, conveys a feeling of nearness or oneness with distant sprawling galaxies, quasars, and black holes.

Perhaps a word of explanation is in order for the

hubris of writing a history of the universe. Having shown that life is a property of planets rather than of organisms has opened the way to thinking of life as a property of the solar system, of the galaxy, or even a feature of the universe. Also some clues about life and mind begin to emerge from our study of biology, and it may be that the mind that emerges on the earth is somehow related to a more cosmic mind. We undertake our study of the history of the universe in order to place our living planet in a larger setting. If there is hubris it is in the arrogance of passionately wanting to know who we are.

The day following the hike I start my writing early in the morning to avoid working in the heat of the afternoon. I sit at my writing desk with aching leg muscles and begin a capsule history of the universe from the big bang until now. If the task is overwhelming, at least the goal is a noble one. Each epoch will not receive equal time. After all, Steven Weinberg wrote a luminous account of "the first three minutes" when so much of cosmic importance presumably transpired. In fact, after reviewing this beginning, much of the next chapter shall be devoted to those later years when the world stood on the brink of life's origin.

Of course, what is written here is not history, observed by men and women and then recorded. One is reminded of the words to Job from out of the whirlwind: "Where were you when I laid the foundations of the earth? Tell me, if you have understanding." What I write is far from traditional history, nevertheless it is not without standing. The strategy is to reconstruct the unfolding of the universe according to our best judgment, based on modern science and supported by experimental evidence. What one writes is a scenario, but it is not a creation legend. At every sentence the script is limited by the laws of nature and observations of today's universe. It certainly is not truth with a capital T, but it is the best that can be done at the moment, and it is powerful. In more religious terms, the most sacred gift that has been bestowed on us is a mind capable of struggling to understand the world in which we live, its past and present and perhaps its future. That mind is also capable of seeking for purpose, and that search becomes our joyous burden.

Each age according to its understanding records its vision of the beginning and, in some cases, of the end. The story may change very fast nowadays, but Rabbi Hillel's words ring out on this one: "It is not up to you to finish the task. Neither are you free to keep from working on it. And if not now, when?" Part of our humanity is to understand who we are, where we have come from, and whither we are going. Spinoza and Einstein declare that bending our intellects to that task can be a sacred act.

In these terms the book *The First Three Minutes*, by Steven Weinberg, is one of the most special; for it is the story of what happened in the earliest time of our current universe some 15 to 20 billion years ago. What makes this work so exciting is not its truth or falsity; I am in no position to judge. The book is thrilling because it informs us that mankind in general and physicists in particular have learned so much about the physical world that it is meaningful to calculate and speculate about the early seconds of this universe's existence. We have been able to construct theories so powerful that they can take us back 15 billion years and make assertions that are subject to experimental test today. This understanding, as well as discoveries in other fields, gives an indication of the glory of the human mind and suggests still more.

To put it in the perspective of the last three hundred years, a very short time, we started with Newton's laws of motion and theory of universal gravitation, which enabled us to understand how bodies can interact over vast distances. This made sense of the complex motions of the solar system. In the 1800s we developed theories concerning thermodynamics, statistical mechanics, electromagnetism, and the radiation laws, which allowed us more perceptively to see how matter and radiation interact and to understand the meaning of that enormously powerful concept of temperature. This made it possible to develop the earth sciences in terms of their physical foundations.

Early in the twentieth century, the development of Einstein's theory of relativity allowed us to begin formulating large-scale models of the universe. We learned about radioactivity and nuclear reactions and now can understand how stars are formed and how they can generate the energy to shine for billions of years. We learned about quantum mechanics, so that now we can interpret the spectral distribution of light coming from distant stars.

And then came the modern period of high-energy nuclear physics and the world of leptons, baryons, and quarks. With the data of astrophysics and the fundamental understanding of matter and energy, found by going from observation to constructs to observation, one is able to formulate a theory of the earth's beginning. Weinberg's approach is not just an abstract theory, for it predicts spectroscopic shifts in the light from distant galaxies, it predicts the background electromagnetic radiation filling all of intergalactic space, and it predicts the cosmic abundances of hydrogen and helium. These are testable predictions that form a tight loop of understanding.

The First Three Minutes is a view of the beginning. It starts at one-hundredth of a second into the big bang. The temperature is 100 billion degrees, and there is an incredibly dense array of electrons, positrons, photons, neutrinos, antineutrinos, and a much smaller number of protons and neutrons. Weinberg does not carry the picture back to an earlier time because present-day physics is inadequate. In any case, it is true that any model can be taken back to a point about which we have nothing to say. We come to either an infinitely oscillating universe or one that, once born, will flourish for a while and then perish. These are equally incomprehensible concepts, at the limit of human understanding. It is said that someone once asked Saint Augustine, "What was God doing before he created time?" The sage paused and then replied, "He was creating hell for people who ask questions like that."

In any case, at one-hundredth of a second into the big bang we have a very hot, very rapidly expanding universe, which Weinberg described as an undifferentiated soup of matter and energy at a temperature of 100 billion degrees. Electrons, positrons, photons, neutrinos, and antineutrinos predominate, but the density is so high that even the existence of particles is hard to comprehend. The next view given is at 0.21 seconds. The temperature has dropped to 30 billion degrees, particles are appreciably farther apart, and neutrons and protons are discernible. The next act in the epic is at 1.09 seconds and a mere 10 billion degrees. The interactions between neutrinos and other particles have almost ceased, and the density of matter is down to 380,000 grams per cubic centimeter. To visualize that density, imagine a large motorcycle compacted down into a little cube less than one-half inch on a side.

The universe continues its expansion but at a slower rate. At 13.83 seconds the temperature is 3 billion degrees and stable nuclei like helium are beginning to form.

And so the processes continue until, after 700,000 years, the universe is cool enough for stable atoms to form, and all the ordinary matter is a mass of turbulent, expanding gas consisting of about three-fourths hydrogen and one-fourth helium. Out of this swirling, turbulent mass comes the next stage, the formation of galaxies, stars, and the atoms necessary for life.

Before going on, I must pause and argue a bit with Professor Weinberg. Because his work is such a paean to human intellectual possibilities, it was rather shocking to come, on the last page, to the following thought:

> It is almost irresistible for humans to believe that we have some special relation to the universe, that human life is not just a more-or-less farcical outcome of a chain of accidents reaching back to the first three minutes, but that we were somehow built in from the beginning. As I write this I happen to be in an airplane at 30,000 feet, flying over Wyoming en route home from San Francisco to Boston. Below, the earth looks very soft and comfortable—fluffy clouds here and there, snow turning pink as the sun sets, roads stretching straight across the country from one town to another. It is very hard to realize that this all is just a tiny part of an overwhelmingly hostile universe. It is even harder to realize that this present universe has evolved from an unspeakably unfamiliar early condition, and faces a future extinction of endless cold or intolerable heat. The more the universe seems comprehensible, the more it also seems pointless.

In the first place, it is not credible to assert that a universe that can produce a Steven Weinberg is pointless. Secondy, I want to argue against cosmic hubris. Human life spans are three score and ten years or a bit more. We live in a universe about 15 billion years old on a planet about 4.5 billion years of age, and are members of a species less than 2 million years old that has spent only about ten thousand years thinking about itself and its world. To be downbeat about events in the far distant future is to underestimate our ability to look ahead. Yes,

I know that in 8 billion years the sun will become a red giant and toast my favorite objects to cinders or even less recognizable things. But in 8 billion years or even 8 million years it is unlikely that my descendants will even be *Homo sapiens*. To engage in weltschmerz about billion-year time-scale problems is to turn our backs on present joy and responsibility. To me part of that joy and responsibility is to understand the universe. Given the wonder of that universe, it seems wrong to focus on its alleged pointlessness. Existence is point enough; everything else is a bonus.

An anecdote best expresses my feeling.

Back in graduate school days, Lucille and I had recently moved into an apartment and were being joined for dinner by a friend who was a fellow graduate student. He was depressed from thinking about the second law of thermodynamics and the eventual heat death of the universe. My ratiocination was of no avail in shaking our friend loose from despair. But then the lasagna Lucille had been preparing arrived with a bottle of Chianti. We sat down to eat and his gloom disappeared in a social evening spent discussing things that we could do something about.

Assertions of pointlessness are a supreme challenge to the gift of existence. Whether they come from Schopenhauer, Sartre, or Weinberg, they must be taken with a grain of salt. These defenders of the pointless have spent lives working hard to make a point, and their very lives are examples of meaning in our finite world of human culture.

Let's return to the early universe in the first few million years. It was largely composed of photons, hydrogen atoms, helium atoms, neutrinos, and antineutrinos all moving apart as the consequence of the big bang. But for one factor the system would simply keep untangling forever. There is, however, the universal force of gravitation between all matter. Gravity is still among the least understood forces in physics, yet for those of us who see more than just randomness in the world, a force that draws things together is understandable, even necessary.

This gathering of matter around local agglomerations leads to condensed objects forming in large swirling clouds, or nebulae, and collections of particles within these superstructures condensing into stars and star clusters. In time some of the stars blow up and explode, spewing intergalactic dust. Gravitational attraction takes over and new centers form, giving rise to second-generation stars made from hydrogen and helium and the debris of first-generation stars. This process continues generating stars, planets, star clusters, pulsars, black holes, and all of the other strange mélange of celestial objects. The process always involves gravity locally overcoming the dispersive force of the big bang and subsequent smaller explosions, and gathering particles together. As the matter condenses, it warms up because gravitational potential is converted into heat. At high enough temperatures the nuclei are moving fast enough for fusion reactions to take place, further heating the system and synthesizing new nuclei, new chemical elements. And so the galaxy evolves.

Our early galaxy, like the rest of the universe, started as a collection of hydrogen and helium atoms. Spinning from an initial angular momentum, the galaxy condenses, flattening under gravitational attraction along the axis of spin while condensing less slowly in the radial direction where centrifugal and centripetal forces tend to balance. An analogy might clarify this notion. Consider a mass of pizza dough held together by its inherent stickiness and spun by the baker around an axis of rotation. The stickiness keeps it compact along the axis where centrifugal forces expand the dough at right angles to the axis. The resulting object achieves a disk shape out of the same kind of balance of forces that determines the structure of galaxies. Within this spinning, saucerlike galaxy local aggregates of matter begin to form into stars, which are believed to occur in clusters of hundreds or thousands.

As a star the size of the sun begins to form, it is at first a large low-density object with a radius about ten thousand times that of the present-day sun. The protostar shrinks, becomes denser, and heats up to about 4,000° surface temperature. This temperature is then maintained while the interior heats up. At the critical temperature, nuclear fusion reactions begin, which produce more energy, and the star heats up to almost 6,000° surface temperature, where it remains in a steady state for a long time. The primary fusion reaction involves four hydrogens condensing to form a helium and releasing large quantities of energy. At this stage in the life of a star its temperature is effectively maintained by the burning of nuclear fuel.

The fusion of hydrogen is the reaction we are trying to carry out in a controlled way for use as an energy source. We are some years away from the engineering solution of commercially feasible fusion reactors. The hydrogen fusion reaction is the same one that takes place in the explosive release of energy in a hydrogen bomb, but operating it in a controlled manner is much more difficult.

The initial mass that begins to condense when a protostar forms depends on detailed local conditions in the galaxy. The larger the condensing mass the hotter the star that forms and the more quickly it burns up. There is a classification system of stars that largely depends on the nature of the light they emit. As already noted, "The color of a star, you can be sure, is mainly due to its temperature." Stars are thus classified as types O, B, A, F, G, K, M, ranging from the hottest, O types, to the coldest, M types. Our sun is a G-type star.

The question of why large stars burn out faster is at first puzzling. Although they give out energy faster, they contain more fuel, so one might expect the two factors to balance. The answer is quantitative; a star 100 times as massive as the sun radiates energy 100,000 times as fast and thus lasts only one-thousandth as long.

After stars of the solar type burn in a steady state for many billions of years, they use up their primary fuel and go through another set of nuclear reactions, leading the outer shell to expand and cool. They become red giants and explode, spewing out cosmic debris. The still-burning core is left as a white dwarf, which then ages continually cooling down to the temperature of intergalactic space. Astronomer Carl Sagan has described this process: "A typical star begins life auspiciously, as a bright yellow giant, and then metamorphoses, in early adolescence, into a yellow dwarf. After spending most of its life in this state, the yellow dwarf rapidly expands into a luminous red giant . . . and decays violently into a hot white dwarf. It ends its life, cooling inexorably, as a degenerate black dwarf."

Thus, just as people are born, age, live, and die, so it is for islands, for stars, and maybe for universes. When I previously mentioned middle-aged tourists on a middle-aged island, I should have added they were being warmed by a middle-aged star.

The energy radiated by stars thus comes from gravitational potential and the nuclear energy of fusion reactions. In the very young universe the only elements were hydrogen and helium from the big bang, so that all the early reactions had to use this basic primordial material. Fusion then produces heavier elements, so that the same reactions that power the stars result in the synthesis of all the elements of the periodic table. The processes responsible for stellar energy are also responsible for the existence of the elements out of which the earth is made. Tying energy sources to informational structures also occurs in metabolism and seems to be a general feature of the universe. The elements other than hydrogen and helium are not the primordial stuff of the universe: they were cooked up in the interior of stars as part of the energy-generating process.

As red giants shed the products of their burning into space, the galaxy then contains atoms of carbon, oxygen, and nitrogen as well as hydrogen, helium, and small amounts of other elements. As second-generation stars begin to condense from this material, the evolution of the star is more complex because of the richer variety of elements. Some typical reactions in the generation of atomic nuclei are:

$$3(^4\text{He}) \rightarrow {}^{12}\text{C} + \text{Energy}$$
$$^{12}\text{C} + {}^4\text{He} \rightarrow {}^{16}\text{O} + \text{Energy}$$
$$2(^{12}\text{C}) \rightarrow {}^{24}\text{Mg} + \text{Energy}$$
$$2(^{12}\text{C}) \rightarrow {}^4\text{He} + {}^{20}\text{Ne} + \text{Energy}$$

The superscripts before the letters are the automatic weights of the isotopes. In the first reaction three heliums come together to form a carbon atom. In the second a carbon and helium nucleus merge to produce an oxygen, and in the third two carbon nuclei coalesce to either stay together as a magnesium or come apart as a helium and a neon. All of these nuclear fusion reactions have been carried out in high-energy nuclear accelerators such as cyclotrons and synchrotrons and are rather well understood. Second-generation stars are made of primordial hydrogen and helium as well as the debris of first-generation stars. They start out with some appreciable quantity of higher-atomic-weight elements and thus support fusion reactions, leading to even higher atomic weights. Second-generation stars may also explode, giving off debris that can form into third-

generation stars. There are some of these stellar grand-
children around but likely few great-grandchildren; the
universe isn't old enough. With each generation the
amount of high-atomic-number material increases.

There are two impressive generalizations from our
very brief recounting of material on the formation and
decay of galaxies and stars. The first is that the mind of
man contemplating falling apples and nuclear physics
has been able to produce a very convincing picture of
what goes on in the universe at large and even what
goes on in the deep interior of very distant stars. The
second conclusion is that the very atoms out of which
we are made were cooked up at incredible temperatures
in stellar interiors. They are the residue of the nuclear
burning of the primordial hydrogen and helium that
emerged from the big bang. I see myself on the one side
reaching back into the interior of stars that bred me and
on the other reaching into exquisite mental processes
that comprehend that stellar inferno. If all of that makes
one something of a mystic, I think it should.

I sometimes go walking through the woods in the
suburbs of New Haven. That, too, evokes the same
brand of mysticism.

Woodbridge

These woods,
Are my church in chronicles
The synagogue of my alienation
The temple of my contemplation
The mosque of my unmasking

The fallen trees tell me of dying
The rotting logs reassure me that
I too will be cycled and recycled
Down the megaseconds of time

The winter woods are my covenant with death
They speak the silence of sleep beneath a blanket of snow
They are my tie with those whose lives touched mine
Before they too slept under a blanket of silence

The spring woods are my promise
I cannot discern the nature of that hope
Yet I can feel within my cells the radiation of growth
The strength of other cells reviving and dividing

The summer woods are my doxology
Praising the power of living
In a cacophony of chirping, cheeping,
Rustling, crackling, hooting and peeping.

The autumn woods have a different message
They announce the coming of the end
In an art form so full of splendor
That the end itself seems like an act of nature's wisdom

The floor of the forest, decaying leaves
Whose dissolution tells
That man is a dissipative instability
A vortex among vortices, whose atoms
Were once cooked in the interior of a giant star
And may one day reside in a white dwarf or a black hole
Until cosmic processes upset even these structures
In times too far distant to contemplate

The ceiling of the woodland, open sky
Alternately giving the light of sun and taking heat at night
In a diurnal reminder of the cycles
And cycles of cycles and cycles of cycles of cycles
Which are but part of the continuing mystery

Standing among my trees, shrubs, mammals, reptiles, and
*   insects*
I cannot fathom the existence of existence
But only feel the flow of a universe
Whose innermost secrets I will never know

Although it seems strange at first, we know far more about the formation of stars than we do about the formation of planets. In part this is because there are limitless stars available to study and take measurements of while there is only one solar system we have been able to observe. Our observations of all but one planet have been, until recent years, extremely limited. While astronomers suspect that many if not most F- and G-type stars have solar systems, that is inferred from stellar spectra, and direct sightings are not available. We thus have to reason from our own planetary system and the laws of physics.

That reliance on physics means that in discussing the next stage in our history of the universe we have to talk about angular momentum (that is another one of those phrases that sometimes gets you treated as if you were someone to avoid). First let's review the situation. Our universe formed about 15 billion years ago in an absolutely mind-boggling cataclysm. It went through an enormous expansion for the first few hundred million years or so. Then for the next 10 billion years, more or less, galaxies formed, stars evolved and blew up or burned out. In the debris from all that action, and using leftover primordial hydrogen and helium, our sun and solar system formed under the influence of gravitation. This was about 5 billion years ago.

Now back to angular momentum. All spinning objects possess a tendency to keep rotating that is called angular momentum and depends on the speed of rotation and the distance of the center of mass from the axis about which the object is spinning. Angular momentum is conserved; in an isolated system once you've got it, you've got it. To get rid of it you have to interact with another system. Let's look at an example we've all seen. If you have a spinning ice skater with her hands spread out, as she brings her hands down by her side she starts spinning faster and faster. What happens is this: the mass of her arms gets closer to the axis of spinning, so in order to conserve angular momentum she starts spinning faster. As she raises her arms she slows down. Friction complicates the story but need not bother us when dealing with spinning solar systems.

Now consider the rotating contracting protostar. As material condenses, it gets closer to the spinning axis, and the rotational speed picks up. This conserves angular momentum. But because of magnetic forces the quantity can be conserved in another way. These magnetic interactions cause the outer material to start spinning faster while the inner star core slows down. This keeps all the material from gravitationally collapsing into the star, and the rotating bands, which may at first look like the rings of Saturn, condense into planets and keep spinning around the star, thus preserving the amount of angular momentum.

So the star and its planetary system simultaneously form in a way consistent with the conservation of angular momentum. The atoms do not distribute quite uniformly, so that the inner planets are dense and have more heavy atoms than the outer ones. In any case, the planets that have only 1/700 of the mass of the solar system possess more than 98 percent of the angular momentum.

More than 4.5 billion years ago one of the spinning inner rings condensed into the planet Earth. The materials out of which the planet formed were small particles, called planetesimals, which were made mostly of silicon, oxygen, iron, and magnesium, with small amounts of all the other elements. Once the material randomly accreted it underwent a meltdown due to two energy sources: the conversion of gravitational energy to heat, and the heat generated by the disintegration of radioactive elements. When the temperature got high enough to melt the iron, this denser metal moved under the influence of gravity toward the center, giving rise to the molten iron core and displacing the lighter material upward. This planetary differentiation resulted in the layers we talked about when we were walking on the lithosphere. The iron core also gives rise to the earth's magnetic field.

The early hot planet contained no oceans or atmospheres, for the planetesimals out of which it condensed were far too small to gravitationally hold liquids or gases. However, in the meltdown and differentiation stage steam issued forth with hot lava to give rise to oceans and continents. Carbon dioxide, methane, ammonia, hydrogen, and nitrogen were released to form the primitive atmosphere. The atmosphere and hydrosphere thus evolved slowly by an outgassing of the planet. About 3.6 billion years ago the earth had settled down to something we might recognize—land and water and some kind of atmosphere. That atmosphere lacked free oxygen and therefore lacked ozone to filter the sun's ultraviolet. The powerful, intense radiation of the atmosphere caused vigorous photochemical activity and gave rise to the early chemical cycles.

The planet was lifeless but chemically active and hovered on the brink of life. Rocks from 400 million years later (3.2 billion years ago) have what appear to be fossil remains of primitive life forms; descendants of the very earliest cells. There is apparently a relatively short time between the cooling from the meltdown and the origin of life; perhaps the processes coexisted in time. All of this temporal overlap is to suggest that the coming of life is a natural part of the evolution of this our planet rather than some freak accident, as insisted on by those who resist enjoying being part of the natural history of the universe.

CHAPTER 14

The Origin of Life

Reconstructing the major transitions in cosmic history is a very difficult task, for each large-scale advance tends to destroy evidence of the previous state. The big bang clearly obliterated prior details, and the formation of the sun and the planets erased much evidence about the earlier swirling nebula that gave rise to them. In a similar way life has so altered planetary chemistry that recovering the detailed description of the planet before biogenesis poses difficult problems.

To achieve a convincing theory for the formation of the earliest organisms on earth there are two approaches. We can start with the properties of present-day organisms and our knowledge of fossils and work our way back through the history of the planet, or we can start with the nature of atoms and molecules and the geology of the early planet and work our way forward. The first approach begins with the taxonomic tree of life and the generalizations of molecular biology and moves toward trying to reconstruct the nature of the earliest organisms. Alternatively, physics, chemistry, and planetary science can be taken as starting points in an attempt to formulate a logical scenario leading to biogenesis. The second approach is similar to the one used in trying to construct the first 10 billion years. In a completely successful formulation the two approaches will end up telling the same story.

There are a number of idiosyncratic underlying beliefs about this problem of the origin of life and I'd better make them explicit at the beginning. First, when I say "origin of life," I refer to the beginnings of cellular life. Cells are, for this purpose, membrane-bounded self-replicating entities. Other life forms are conceptually possible, as can be vividly seen in the work of science fiction writers, and the early history of the earth could have involved some self-replicating chemical reactions outside of cells. But the life we know with certainty is cellular in nature, and that feature also characterizes the fossil record for as far back as we can take it. I'm going to end up with the view that life is ultimately a property of planets, but it manifests itself through the activity of cells.

A second assumption is that cellular life on this planet originated right here from material in the original condensate. The other possibility is that life migrated here from somewhere else in the universe. There is, however, no experimental evidence for interstellar living forms, although the word "panspermia" has been coined to describe such objects. One shouldn't get confused and believe that a word guarantees the existence of an object, even though the medieval logicians spent a lot of time debating the issue. Since I am arguing that life is a planetary property, there is no necessity to look for a mysterious origin or seeding. Rather, we must study the evolution of the planet from inorganic to living forms. The biosphere and other geospheres are so uniquely interrelated that it seems to violate Occam's razor to seek independent origins. In any case, immigration does not solve the basic problem of life's origin but only moves the locale for considering how cells arose to Krypton, or spiral galaxy 1781, or wherever the panspermia supposedly came from.

Another tacit assumption is that the origin of cellular life is an accessible scientific problem. That does not mean that it is solved but that it is in principle solvable using methods that characterize the scientific approach. New laws and theories may be sought, but they will be of the same philosophical (epistemological) character as existing laws of science. We discussed this in talking about the loop of verification, and I'm betting that the same mode of reasoning can be applied to understanding the origin of life.

A number of scientists believe that the origin required so many chance events of such low probability that we have no way of studying it within the framework of science, even though it involved perfectly normal laws of nature. According to this view, the origin can be studied only as a problem in history, an unfolding in time whose traces have been all but obliterated by subsequent events. The chance postulate denies the possibility of investigating the problems in the laboratory. The assumption of accessibility, on the other hand, provides an intellectual climate for exploring the problem to its limits.

The view that life's origin cannot be predicted from physics because of the dominance of chance factors was elaborated by Jacques Monod in his book *Chance and Necessity*. This is our second attack on that viewpoint and another is forthcoming. The randomness Monod discussed was due largely to genetic mutations, but he also extrapolated back to the prebiotic chemical epoch— the period before life began on earth. In disagreement with Monod, I'm convinced that many of the features leading up to life can be predicted from physics. It is premature to rule out life as a deterministic rather than a chance phenomenon, particularly since we are only beginning to develop those branches of physical science necessary to study the problem. The assertion that biogenesis can never be predicted from first principles is a self-fulfilling prophecy because is discourages us from the hard work necessary to pursue the problem to its limit. Science is a young enterprise.

I wonder about scientists who assume that the unknown is unknowable because they don't know it. It's important to keep stressing that human culture and intellectual pursuits are only about ten thousand years old. We're not at the end of understanding; we're somewhere near the beginning. In a 15-billion-year-old universe, our efforts to comprehend the meaning of that universe have occupied only slightly over one one-millionth of the total time. Indeed, there is excitement in the thought of all that remains to be discovered. Each succeeding year will increase our understanding of the universe. The study of science insofar as it seeks that understanding is a mystical pursuit or a religious act. Albert Einstein once made a very forceful statement of this viewpoint. He wrote: "I want to know how God created the universe. I am not interested in this or that spectral line or other phenomenon, I want to know God's mind. The rest are details."

Now we can get on with starting from present-day biology. Let's recall the tree of life we've all seen prominently displayed in natural history museums and biology textbooks. Up at the top branches, if the scheme were to be presented in full detail, would be the two million or so contemporary species that can be studied in the laboratory or in the field. At the bottom are the very earliest forms, presumably resembling the cellular life that existed in the time following life's origin.

The great division among present life forms is between the procaryotes and eucaryotes. The procaryotes are unicellular and lack membrane-covered organelles such as nuclei. They include bacteria, blue-green algae, methane bacteria, and mycoplasma. The relationships of these organisms are unclear, but there is no doubt that procaryotes form a cohesive group distinct from all other organisms in their organization. The eucaryotes are characterized by internal organelles such as energy-transforming mitochondria, food-producing chloroplasts, and nuclei. They also have chromosomes and undergo the elaborate processes of meiosis characteristic of those structures. The eucaryotes include plants, animals, algae, fungi, and protozoa. All living organisms are included in the procaryotes and eucaryotes.

Because of their greater simplicity it is widely assumed that the procaryotes preceded the eucaryotes, and the next step back in time would be the ancestors of these unicellular forms. While this seems highly likely, we cannot rule out the possibility that eucaryotes came first, or that both forms had a common ancestor that was neither procaryote nor eucaryote.

Given this elaborate tree of life and the enormous number of present-day forms, we are nevertheless presented with a strategy. It is clear that cellular and biochemical structures that are common to all living cells must have been present in the earliest forms. How else could they have become distributed among all current organisms? Thus we are asserting that ubiquitous structures and common functions are probably primitive. These features that characterize all life as we know it then constitute the irreducible minimum specifications of all life. The features had to exist at the root of the tree. We are in a position to move from studies in the laboratory to a reconstruction of cells three and one-half billion years ago. That's an exciting concept.

The boundary that separates each cell from its surroundings is the plasma membrane, a closed skin about one ten-millionth of an inch in thickness. The membrane is largely made up of special part-lipid (oily), part-polar (water-loving, or *hydrophilic*) molecules that fit together in a natural and structural pattern. The membrane forms a very thin, oily layer made of the lipid portions of the molecules, and this barrier separates the watery interior of the cell from the watery exterior. On the average the membrane is the thickness of two polar-lipid molecules and is called a *bimolecular leaflet* structure. Such aggregates require molecules with long, thin, oily parts attached to a water-loving group. The gathering of these molecules into a sheetlike structure is the universal physical process used in constructing biological membranes.

The essential job of a membrane is to separate a cell from its suroundings. The membrane defines a living entity by providing a boundary that forms a barrier to the free flow of molecules. Present-day membranes have numerous proteins associated with the structural polar lipids. Primordial membranes may have been constructed almost entirely of polar-lipid molecules and thus may have lacked many of the associated proteins. We'll have more to say about this when we come back to our scenario of the first protocell.

One thing can be said about membranes—they are almost a fourth state of matter. With respect to solubility, in a watery world everything is, for deep physical reasons depending on electrical charge distribution in atoms and molecules, either hydrophobic or hydrophilic. This major physical distinction is the guiding principle in the building of membranes. Thus these structures are of rather natural occurrence in the evolution of the planet; they result from certain fundamental properties of molecules. On the surface and within the membrane, proteins are responsible for catalyzing chemical reactions, transporting materials in and out of the cell, and changing energy into chemically useful forms. This talk about cellular energy reminds me of something that happened many years back.

I was being interviewed by a reporter from a national news magazine and the interchange went badly. Every time I mentioned adenosine triphosphate the reporter balked, and we had to go back to square one. The resulting article was garbled and gave a confused account of the research in progress. The lesson I learned was "stay away from big words and be careful of what you say to reporters." The troubling issue persisting over the years is that one of the great intellectual triumphs of all time, the understanding of energy and metabolism and its great uniformity among all species, is written in tongue-twisting polysyllabic words, such as nicotinamide-adenine-dinucleotide-phosphate. The most significant advances in understanding the nature of life remain unknown to most people because the concepts are inseparable from very long words that intimidate the uninitiated and keep them from insights that hold a wide range of unexplored implications.

But enter almost any biochemistry or molecular biology laboratory and you are sure to find posted on the walls or doors four or more printed sheets bearing a connected graph of all the major biochemical reactions that living organisms carry out in their cells. The chart is a great synthesis, a set of generalizations summing up experiments by generations of workers. It can be compared to other great achievements of the human intellect, such as the periodic table of the elements or the Linnaean system of classifying species.

To envision intermediary metabolism in proper perspective, we start with the view of biology as unity within diversity. Variety is clearly evident in the array of plants and animals that greet the eye wherever we look. Diversity is one of those indisputable facts of life. Unity begins to emerge when we penetrate beneath the surface to the intracellular machinery and processes used by species to grow and reproduce. An examination at the microscopic and molecular levels reveals common features of cell and organelle structure. We've talked about this earlier, but it deserves another look.

Continuing down the size range from organisms to molecules, we come to intermediary biochemistry, a collection of hundreds or thousands of enzymatic reactions by which a cell shapes matter and energy into forms useful for its own purposes. Here we sense the full impact of unity; the single *Chart of Intermediary Metabolism* applies with equal validity to all the species that inhabit the planet. The core set of biochemical reactions of any organism from a bacterium to a great blue whale is found on the chart. No organism employs the full set, but each species uses some substantial part of the reactions shown. What may be alarmingly complex to students studying for an examination becomes remarkably unifying and almost simple when we realize that it encompasses all of the diverse flora and fauna coexisting in the biosphere.

When we search for further unifying features, they are not hard to find. Almost every sequence of metabolic processes involves one or more reactions with molecules of adenosine triphosphate (reporter from my youth, please note). This ubiquitous substance, best known by its abbreviation, ATP, is central to energy processing in all cells. We find ATP printed along practically every line in the metabolic chart. If it were represented only once in our network of biochemical pathways, the drawing would be a giant rosette with all lines passing through the center. ATP is the final energy-transfer molecule in almost every cellular process. The reactions of this compound heat our bodies, power our muscles, charge our nerves, and otherwise drive the processes of life.

When we inquire how ATP is made, we find three universal methods: It is produced by a certain few chemical reactions within the cell; it is produced at membranes where the final burning (oxidation) of foodstuffs takes place; it is produced by photosynthetic reactions occurring at membranes. The major sources of all reactions producing ATP and incorporating available energy in that molecule occur at membranes where electrochemical events separate ions and store electrical energy as if the membranes were miniature capacitors. This stored energy is that used to make adenosine triphosphate from its low-energy building blocks, adenosine diphosphate and phosphate. There is a close association between membranes and ATP.

Genetics provides a further example of unity. Inside every cell is the coding material made up of molecules of deoxyribonucleic acid, or DNA. Each DNA in the cell is a double helix consisting of two long polymeric molecules twisted around each other in snakelike form, like the caduceus, or physician's symbol. Each of the polymers is a sequence of repeating molecular groupings, called monomers, strung together in a chain. DNA is made up of four monomers, nucleotides that carry the coding groupings: adenine (A), guanine (G), cytosine (C), and thymine (T). The order in which the monomers are strung together in one of the chains (for example, AGCCTTAGCGATT . . .) constitutes the genetic message, and the total sequence, millions of monomers in length, constitutes the hereditary information. The two DNA chains are twisted around each other and are complementary, meaning each A is paired with a T on the other chain and each G is paired with a C. The hereditary information thus exists as a long sequence of symbols.

Within each cell are several kinds of ribonucleic acids (RNA), which serve as intermediates between the information of DNA and the structure and function of proteins. There are long, thin polymeric-messenger RNAs made of single strands of sequences of monomers, which carry the coding groupings: adenine, guanine, cytosine, and uracil (U). The single-stranded macromolecules carry the cell's genetic information from the genes (DNA) to the structural and functional molecules of protein. A sequence of three nucleotides in the RNA specifies an amino acid in the proteins. The latter are polymers of amino acids in a chain. Cells contain transfer RNAs to mediate between the coding triplets in the messenger RNAs and the amino acids in solution. The cells also contain ribosomes, tiny factories made of RNAs and proteins. The ribosomes are the actual sites of action for reading out the messages and assembling the proteins.

In every living cell are a collection of proteins, which are the workhorses of the system. Their structures are specified by the messages in the DNA, and they act in two ways: by catalyzing almost all the chemical reactions that take place and by serving as structural components. The chemical reactions of the cell generally have two purposes: either to convert energy into biologically useful forms or to synthesize molecules needed for the structure and function of the cell. Amino acids and nucleotides are among the kinds of molecules that must be produced by the system in order to synthesize new polymers. The reaction networks are exquisitely interrelated so as to optimize the value of ingested molecules in the overall economy.

The syntheses of macromolecules of DNA, RNA, and protein from their building blocks are highly interrelated processes. Starting from a double-stranded DNA molecule, with its pair of chains, two possible processes occur: the two strands may unwind, and each may act as a template for the formation of a new strand. This occurs by the attraction of complementary nucleotides from solution, followed by an enzymatic joining of the attracted nucleotides into a new strand. This synthesis leads to two identical double-stranded DNA molecules, each containing the complete hereditary information, and constitutes the process of replication of genetic material. One double-stranded DNA molecule has given rise to two double-stranded molecules each identical to the original.

Alternatively, one strand of the DNA may act as a template for the synthesis of its complementary single-stranded RNA. This RNA is released and acts as a messenger specifying the sequence of amino acids in proteins. Protein synthesis occurring at ribosomes is a complex process requiring ATP, amino acids, and activating enzymes in solution, as well as other enzymes that function at the ribosomal surface. The synthesized macromolecules include both cellular enzymes and structural proteins. The steps in macromolecular synthesis are now known in exquisite detail. We will forgo the description of this detail in order to move on with the problem of the origin of life.

The biochemical steps just briefly listed appear to be an irreducible minimum set of operations for modern organisms. All present-day living forms grow and replicate using the same molecular mechanisms and the same basic pathways. The unity-within-diversity has its most fundamental basis in this ubiquitousness of molecular hardware and chemical reactions in all living things.

Given the previous series of generalizations as defining contemporary life, we can then go on to ask, What is the simplest present-day embodiment of these generalizations? What is the simplest living cell, the minimum free-living organism? To get personal again, I want to say that the search for the smallest cell is not just an abstraction to me. It was sufficiently important that I spent ten years defining, studying, and characterizing these microorganisms. They may be more complex than the first cells, but their complexity establishes an upper limit for the sophistication of primordial systems.

Since all hereditary information in procaryotes is linearly encoded in DNA genomes, the modern free-living organism with the smallest genome may be presumed to be the simplest one. Intracellular parasites like viruses and rickettsiae are excluded because they must use part of the host cell's genetic information as well as their own.

The search for genetic simplicity led to the mycoplasma, a group of procaryotes lacking a cell wall and of extremely small cell size. Some species have genomes in the neighborhood of 500 million daltons (molecular weight units). On the average, it requires about 800,000 daltons of DNA to encode a single functional protein. Therefore, the smallest known mycoplasmas specify about six hundred biochemical processes. The organism's complexity is limited by the amount of genetic information. The preceding statements on genome size sound very simple, but they are based on three years of hard, skilled, imaginative work by Hans Bode, who first determined these sizes. A substantial number of follow-up studies have confirmed and extended these determinations.

Starting from the outside, the mycoplasma cell is surrounded by a plasma membrane made up of a lipid bilayer, with attached proteins and carbohydrates. Within this membrane is a coiled, closed loop of DNA, containing the cell's entire genetic information. Also found are a few hundred ribosomes, a few thousand protein molecules, and a larger number of ATPs and assorted small molecules.

Calculating theoretically from the known generalizations of molecular biology, the smallest, simplest organism that could carry out absolutely necessary functions of life would require a genome size at least half that of mycoplasma. In other words, *the simplest free-living organisms discovered to date are close to the theoretical limit of simplicity based on the generalizations of molecular biology.* We don't know that mycoplasma are necessarily primitive; they may be degenerate forms of advanced bacteria. They have, however, achieved great simplicity while retaining the ability to exist as free-living forms.

It is possible to extrapolate from the present structure of molecular biology and move back one step toward earlier systems. Since there are viruses that encode their genetic information in double-stranded RNA, and since in principle all known hereditary processes could be carried out using RNA in place of DNA, we can envision an even simpler cell than the existing ones: a cell that uses no DNA. The apparent limit of simplicity would be a mycoplasmalike cell containing double-stranded RNA as the coding material. With such primitive mycoplasmalike organisms as a theoretical minimum living system, let us return to physics and chemistry and ask how such a cell could come about.

Next, we will be still more speculative. What is presented is a best guess based on what I know at the moment. The next trip to the library one island away to read the latest journals could change my mind, so it is well to indicate why this or that assumption is being made. Let the scenario begin.

Go back to the earth four billion years ago. Outgassing has produced oceans, which cover a good deal of the planetary surface. It has also given rise to an atmosphere of nitrogen, ammonia, carbon dioxide, hydrogen, sulfide, water, and other gases. There is little or no free oxygen around. A good deal of volcanic activity exists, with vents both above and below sea level spewing forth molten lava and hot gasses. The day-night cycle is virtually the same as the present except that the day brings more intense solar radiation with a strong ultraviolet component.

Although there are no living cells, a great deal of chemical activity is taking place. The ultraviolet and visible radiation drives photochemical reactions. The lightning, heat from volcanoes, and radioactivity at the surface promote free radical and thermochemical reactions. Free radicals are molecularlike groupings that have one or more broken chemical bonds. They are produced by high energy sources and are extremely chemically reactive. All of these processes have certain chemical products in common, which bear surprising similarity to many present-day biochemicals. A knowledge of these reactions goes back to a series of experiments carried out in 1951.

Stanley Miller was a student working in the laboratory of Nobel laureate Harold Urey, who had postulated that the early atmosphere was rich in hydrogen and poor in oxygen. This meant that oxidation reactions such as combustion and slow burning would not take place. Teacher and student reasoned that in such an environment energy from certain sources could drive the synthesis of organic compounds. Miller set up an experiment to cycle a gas mixture of ammonia, methane, and water through a chamber where a high-voltage electrical spark discharge was maintained. The products of the reaction were trapped by bubbling the gas through water. The results went beyond the expectations of the experimenters. Amino acids and other organic intermediates were formed in substantial quantity.

In the decades following the initial finding, the experiment has been repeated many times. The energy source has been varied from the original spark to ultraviolet radiation, shock waves, heat pulses, alpha-particles, and chemical energy sources. In all cases the product molecules under reducing conditions (little or no oxygen) have included similar biologically interesting compounds.

There are general features of gas-phase compounds of carbon, hydrogen, nitrogen, and oxygen that lead under reducing conditions and high energy flow-throughs to a class of molecules now regarded as biochemicals. The chemistry of these reactions is quite well understood and it all seems straightforward. This means that the right molecules are going to be around as the result of the properties of the periodic table of elements. There is now spectroscopic evidence of organic molecules such as cyanide being widely distributed in the universe. The experiments by Miller and Urey and those that followed have changed our views regarding the molecular components of living systems. We now think of them as being of likely occurrence in our kind of universe.

In the beginning, earth's photochemistry was probably dominated by ultraviolet light. As a result of these processes, molecules were formed that could absorb visible light, and the major component of the sun's radiation was then available to drive chemical reactions.

Looking at the planet as a whole, solar radiation and other energy sources provided for the production of a rich variety of molecules made from simple starting materials like carbon dioxide, nitrogen, ammonia, methane, and water. The complex molecules react with one other in the presence of the available electromagnetic energy and break down into the original simple molecules. There is a simultaneous buildup of complex organic structures and a breakdown of these molecules into their simpler components. This buildup and breakdown constitutes a great cycle of matter driven by a flow-through of energy. This process has many of the features of ecological cycles, except it takes place in the absence of cellular life. Cyclic chemical behavior under energy flow turns out to be a general property of systems under radiation flux and predates life. Indeed, we might think of this prebiological ecology as establishing the physical environment in which life can flourish.

The previous thought deserves some elaboration. If we take any physical system and irradiate it with sufficiently energetic radiation, it will undergo large-scale chemical cycles, from simple low-energy molecules to complex high-energy molecules and then back again. The necessity of such behavior has been demonstrated theoretically in the "cycling theorem." It is proven from physics alone, yet is universally demonstrated on present-day earth in the great ecological cycles. These circular flows predate biology; the early ones were involved in the readying of the earth for the emergence of living forms.

Among the many compounds that occurred on the earth four billion years ago some evidence exists for hydrocarbons, or oils that floated on the surface of the waters. This may come as a shock to environmentalists, but the primordial ocean may have had a surface oil slick. We know that under the influence of ultraviolet radiation some of these molecules are converted to amphiphilic hydrocarbons: molecules with an oily end and a water soluble end. These kinds of molecules will under the right conditions snap together to form membranes. Fragments of this planar membranous material will spontaneously form into closed surfaces and *voilà*, biological individuality has entered the world, for the membrane is a firmament to separate the waters of the cell's interior from the waters of the environment. In more scientific terms, a membranous vesicle impedes the free flow of molecules between the interior and the exterior and thus establishes a space (the cell's interior), or thermodynamic system, within which different chemical processes can occur and reaction products can be retained.

From this perspective the first crucial event in the origin of cellular life is the formation of a plasma membrane, a structure made of amphiphilic molecules, which creates a chemical separation between the interior and the exterior. Because of a focus on life as a property of the evolving planet, I tend not to think about the question of when life began. Rather, the issue is when chemically active, organic cycling systems gave rise to three zones: the inner watery substance, the oily membrane, and the outer watery substance. From a biophilosophical point of view the membrane is the point of interface between the I and the Thou within the realm of existence. Insofar as there is exchange across this membrane, the I and the Thou are connected; insofar as this exchange is restricted, the organism and environment have a certain measure of autonomy.

Once the closed membranous shell forms, a whole series of events become possible that could not have taken place in solution. First, the chemical composition of the interior can be different from the exterior. Second, positive and negative electrical charges can be separated across the membrane as in an electrical capacitor. As a result, a transmembrane electrical potential, or voltage, can be generated, and this voltage can drive electrochemical reactions. Because the flow of electrical current across a membrane can involve either electrons or protons, in addition to the usual electrochemistry, there is a related process, protochemistry, which has recently been shown to be central to biological energy transformation.

In 1978 a British biochemist, Peter Mitchell, was awarded the Nobel Prize for establishing that in photosynthesis and in oxidation reactions in cells the primary process consists of moving protons from one side of the membrane to the other. This transfer produces an electrical charge separation and a change in acidity on the two sides of the membrane. The two effects taken together give rise to what is called an electrochemical potential, which drives protons back across certain channels in the membrane and converts the proton's energy into making ATP. The method of storing energy in cross-membrane potentials has been so broadly demonstrated in all biological taxa that we are now in a position to ask: since it is so ubiquitous, is it primitive? Starting from the theory of evolution, we argue that a ubiquitous feature must be primitive, have independently evolved in every branch of the taxonomic tree, or have universally spread by infection or similar process. The first of these seems most likely, in which case the proton-driven synthesis of energy-storing molecules is primitive.

But could the ever-present ATP molecule have been around in the precellular soup? This is unlikely, but that does not end the story, for the molecule ATP consists of two parts, a complex organic grouping called adenosine and three phosphate groups strung together. The adenosine is involved in signaling an enzymatic specificity, while the energy transformations are entirely in the triphosphate end of the molecule.

$$\text{Triphosphate} + \text{Water} \rightarrow \text{Diphosphate} + \text{phosphate} + \text{energy}$$

Phosphates are perfectly ordinary inorganic molecules that very likely were around in the early days. Hence the original bioenergetics could have utilized inorganic phosphates. And there may be vestiges of this process among the primitive photosynthetic bacteria that even today store energy in the form of polyphosphates, molecules with long chains of phosphate groups. This form of energy storage is also known in other microorganisms.

A notable feature of biochemistry is that most metabolic pathways are governed by phosphate transfer reactions. If the primordial energy source were high-energy polyphosphates, then we would anticipate that the emerging chemical reactions would be dominated by phosphate transfers. In contemporary organisms high-energy ATP is made using oxidation and photosynthesis as energy sources. All subsequent cellular chemistry involves chemical pathways where phosphate groups are transferred from ATP to various organic molecules and subsequent reactions are driven by the energy from the phosphate exchange reactions. Biochemistry is characteristically that subbranch of organic chemistry that is driven by the energy of high-energy phosphate bonds.

Could polyphosphates have been synthesized at an early stage in the development of cells? We can envision a plausible mechanism that operates in much the same manner as today's membrane-associated synthesis of ATP. For among the molecules produced in a Miller-Urey type of synthesis are some that would both absorb visible light and dissolve within the oily parts of membrane vesicles. A vesicle with such molecules dissolved within its membrane would, when exposed to visible light, exhibit a voltage between the outside and inside. This voltage can produce charge separation, and there could be a resultant flow of protons. It has been possible to demonstrate from thermodynamic theory that this flow can be coupled to making polyphosphates. All of the above statements can be justified from well-known physical theory.

In principle, by using known laws of chemistry we envision a primordial cell that absorbs visible light and uses the energy to make high-energy phosphate bonds. Energy stored in these bonds can then selectively direct chemical reactions of the interior along pathways to familiar biological metabolites. The components of the metabolic system could have been selected by the chemical nature of the primary energy source.

All of this is a highly speculative view of the events along the way to cellular life. It does indicate, however, that there are plausible processes, consistent with the known laws of physics and chemistry, that could have given rise to a membrane-bounded vesicle that photosynthetically produces high-energy phosphates and uses this energy to generate some type of metabolic systems.

There is still a long way from this primitive protocell to our postulated minimal contemporary cell whose properties are known from the generalizations of molecular biology. My conjecture is that we will be able to make a case for bridging this gap, but that remains to be done. At the moment there is a missing link between the energy-processing protocell and the genetically sophisticated minimum cell. Jumping that gap, we arrive at conventional evolution, the generation of all the full richness of the taxonomic tree from the first living cells.

There is a little known fact that I think some biologists and geologists would rather keep a secret. Aside from our theoretical biochemical knowledge of early life we have very little idea of what happened to living systems for the first three billion years. Organic life had not discovered shells and bones, so the few fossils that remain come from very special conditions under which cellular remains can be preserved. Almost all the fossils we see in museums are from the past five hundred million years. For the first three billion years life persisted in the ocean; growing, developing, and giving rise to the major groups of animals. During this period photosynthesis developed, along with an oxygen atmosphere, which made possible the rise of land organisms. The life we know is largely from the most recent 15 percent of the life of the planet.

The recent epochs have been extensively studied by biologists and geologists, and two major questions remain: What is the major mechanism of evolution? Does evolution have direction? We'll get back to these when we consider Teilhard de Chardin's vision. First, we'd better take a closer look at what we know about the evolution of modern forms.

CHAPTER 15

The Evolution
of Organic Forms

Anaturalist friend once explained that if Darwin had stopped at the Hawaiian Islands rather than at the Galápagos, he would have found even better evidence for his theory of evolution. For the diversity of the Galápagos finches is far less than the even greater variations of bill shapes among the Hawaiian honeycreepers. The finches provided important clues about the evolving of isolated island populations, and the honeycreepers present even stronger evidence.

For within five million years since their arrival on these islands the original strain of honeycreepers diverged, so that at Darwin's time there were twenty-two highly varied species that occur no place else in the world. "Most remarkable is the great variety in the size and shape of their bills, doubtless in response to the variability of particular types of food."

I'm tempted to drive to Kipahulu or Hosmer Grove to see the crested honeycreeper in order to establish the proper mood to write about evolution, but I'm going to settle for three minutes of meditation while looking at pictures of six species of these avians. The myna birds in the trees along the dock road are acting as acoustical surrogates for the honeycreepers. Actually, our object is not to discuss evolution in any technical sense but to consider the great variety of life forms that have been fruitful and multiplying ever since the earliest cells developed the secret of genetic coding.

Evolution is a subject fraught with difficulty and dispute. It's not that the fact of evolution per se causes trouble among scientists. It's undeniable that countless species have arisen, flourished for a while, and perished, to be replaced by descendent species. What is subject to disagreement is whether the process of species formation is slow and gradual as Darwin maintained or, on a geological time scale, very fast as the modern punctuational model suggests. The latter maintains that over short times, characterized by environmental shifts and isolation of small populations, new species arise quickly and then remain stable for long periods of time. Within any group the evolutionary clock does not run uniformly. It usually just moves along, but periodically it is greatly speeded up.

The word "punctuational" is a terrible affront to the English language, for it suggests asterisks and semicolons rather than brief periods of genetic shift, but we're stuck with the usage of the practitioners in the field. The modern paleontologists, or at least the most vocal among them, find the punctuational model the most satisfactory explanation of their observations. In any case, the fossil record shows periods of intense speciation and periods of slow speciation.

The principal data of evolution consists of collections of fossils. The present theory of evolution is supplemented by genetics, biochemistry, modern relations among species, and the physics of dating samples. Fossils are formed when dead organisms or their parts are preserved in sediments, tars, amber, lava, or other geologically stable forms. Most dead organisms are never fossilized but simply decay away, recycling their atoms into the great global mineral flow patterns. Sometimes the atoms or the organisms are carried away but the shape is preserved by rock formation, as in the petrified forest. Some fossils record only a shape, as in the fascinating dinosaur footprints or the oldest fossil animals known only in impressions from sandstone in South Australia.

The hit-or-miss methods of fossil formation mean that the record of the past is spotty and incomplete. Part of the acrimony surrounding attempts to understand evolution is the fact that the more incomplete the record, the larger the number of possible interpretations. And given a range of interpretation, each theory will find its adherents. We therefore argue our way to consensus. Historians of science delight in telling that consensus is the path to understanding.

With these caveats in mind, it's well to repeat that a recounting of this phase of the planet's history is but a scenario, built on the rocky base of fossils and constrained by our knowledge of the laws of nature. There is nothing wrong with these scripts; it's just that we must be open-minded about rewriting them when new evidence appears or new theoretical knowledge changes the constraints within which we operate.

Evidence points to the origin of modern-day biochemical structures and processes between three and four billion years ago. Great uncertainties exist about that date. There is a scarcity of fossil evidence until about half a billion years ago. That means we know frustratingly little about the first few billion years and a great deal about the last 500 million.

The period from the origin of life until the firm beginnings of the fossil record is called either the Archeozoic Era or the Precambrian. Most biologists assume the earliest organisms were procaryotes, and for the first billion years or so life was dominated by these structurally simple sea-living organisms. Somewhere along the way modern oxygen-generating photosynthesis evolved and the atmosphere began to shift from an oxygen-poor to an oxygen-rich state. Also at some time eucaryotes evolved into more complex single cells than the procaryotes. Eucaryotes possess meiosis and recombination and thus sex entered the world. The exact timing of the development of an oxygen atmosphere, eucaryotes, and animals is very uncertain. In any case, some oxygen in the atmosphere must have been necessary for the first eucaryotes.

From a biological point of view the function of sex is to create new combinations of genes allowing experiments with new phenotypes. These novel phenotypes can be more or less fit, and evolution can run its course in a very speeded-up fashion. After sex was invented, it took a billion years or more to evolve the nerves to know what to do with it.

Toward the end of the Archeozoic Era the seas were inhabited by marine algae, primitive aquatic plants, fungi, protozoa, marine worms, and other invertebrates. Sufficient photosynthesis had occurred to raise the oxygen content of the atmosphere to near present values. Much of this photochemical activity was the result of blue-green algae, which are still a major factor in world-wide oxygen production.

Starting about 500 million years ago in the Cambrian Period we begin to find abundant fossils from a varied collection of phyla including the forerunners of most modern groupings. After three and a half billion years of experimenting with form, shape, and modes of existing, the planet blossoms forth in a brilliant array of species, which constitute the biosphere. At the beginning of the Cambrian Period, plant life is still confined to oceanic algae but most of our present animal phyla have marine representatives. Eight of the nine major invertebrate phyla appear to have representatives that evolved before the beginning of the Cambrian Period or immediately thereafter.

Geologists divide the last half-billion-year period into three subdivisions, the Paleozoic, or Age of Ancient Life, lasting for 300 million years, the Mesozoic, or Age of Reptiles, extending for about 130 million years, and the Cenozoic, or Age of Mammals, covering the past 75 million years. Paleozoic, Mesozoic, and Cenozoic are the eras of documented evolutionary development.

For the first half of the Paleozoic the planet is warm, the great mountains have not yet arisen, and life is mainly in the sea. Algae, fish, trilobites, and corals dominate. Then the land rises; land plants and insects appear about 400 million years ago. Great forests of ferns and conifers grow, readying the land for animal life.

Somewhere early in the Paleozoic some primitive invertebrate line appears to have split into two phyla: echinoderms like starfish and sea urchins; and the first chordates, distinguished by a notochord, the earliest beginnings of a spinal column. We speculate that the line of evolution went from these primitive chordates to agnaths, early jawless fish, which provide the earliest fossils of vertebrates. From the agnaths there was an evolutionary radiation so that by the end of the Paleozoic our planet was inhabited by sharks, bony fish, lungfish, amphibians, and labyrinthodonts, ancestors of the reptiles that came to dominate the Mesozoic Era.

The Mesozoic, or Age of Reptiles, is a time of great geological changes. The originally somewhat flattened lands eventually form into the Andes, Alps, Himalayas, and Rockies. Continents move about under plate tectonics. The fern growths are replaced by gymnosperms, and by the end of the period there are oak and maple forests. The labyrinthodonts, which have been described as looking like stubby-nosed alligators, gave rise late in the Paleozoic to stem reptiles from which radiated the mammallike reptiles, turtles, lizards and snakes, birds and crocodiles and dinosaurs. The dinosaurs rose to dominate earth life and then mysteriously became extinct at the end of the Mesozoic. As descendants of the labyrinthodonts in the modern world we find all the existing terrestrial vertebrates.

The Cenozoic, or last age, represents conditions much closer to those that we now experience. There was the rise of effulgent deciduous forests and then their decline, as in many parts of the world they were replaced by grasslands. The continental drifts established our contemporary global map. The plants and animals in some parts of the world evolved in isolation, as in the Island Continent of Australia or South America before the establishment of the Isthmus of Panama.

The mammals that had begun to speciate late in the Mesozoic began to grow in numbers and kinds to fill all the niches left vacant by the extinction of dinosaurs. The archaic mammals gave rise to marsupials and insectivores. The latter were the beginning of the vast range of placental mammals: the bats, the carnivores, the ungulates, the elephants, the sloths, the whales, the rodents, the rabbits, and the primates. About 40 million years ago the early anthropoids arose. Thirty million years ago there was a rapid evolution of mammalian forms, and by 10 million years before the present time most current species of mammals or their predecessors were extant. The last million years, largely consisting of the Pleistocene Epoch, were characterized by four ice ages and an extensive extinction of mammalian species.

There is little reason to doubt this overall evolutionary

history that has just been sketched so briefly, although we have focused on organisms without considering their relation to and influence on their surroundings.

The evolutionary sweep is so diverse and so many millions of species have played their part that it is well to focus on the underlying unity of biochemical pathways and cellular mechanisms that are propaedeutic to the great diversity of plant and animal forms. A grand question persists. Is there some meaning in all of this great array of form or is blind chance behind the richness and beauty of existence? That indeed is the question.

CHAPTER 16

Teilhard's Vision

Having written our short history of the universe, we come to one of the main reasons for writing it. The time is ripe to focus on the ideas of a man who thought long and hard about that history and concluded that starting from the scientific facts there are conclusions to be drawn of major importance in our understanding of who and what we are.

So for today, I'm especially relieved to be far away from my academic colleagues. In Lahaina it isn't going to bother many people to learn that someone is sitting in the public library agreeing with the vision of Pierre Teilhard de Chardin. His book *The Phenomenon of Man* is on sale at Amy's bookstore and coffeehouse, but it's not a fast-moving item. However, back in America, Teilhard's name is anathema to many scientists. Among contemporary science writers, Teilhard is the least popular major thinker. Stephen Jay Gould, with uncharacteristic criticism, assumes that Teilhard was the chief conspirator in the Piltdown hoax, involving a fraudulent humanoid skull presumably of early man found in 1908 at Piltdown on the southeast coast of England. Jacques Monod speaks of the intellectual spinelessness of Teilhard's philosophy, and Peter Medawar refers to his writing as nonsense tricked out with a variety of metaphysical conceits. These are not just academic jibes, they are karate chops to the back of the intellectual neck.

Why risk the wrath of the scientific community by presenting Teilhard's view? The story began many years ago with the purchase of Teilhard's chief work, *The Phenomenon of Man*, in a bookstore in Grand Central Terminal in New York. The introduction occurred during the bumpy, almost two-hour train ride to New Haven. On arriving home I had trouble leaving that book until I finished it. While it was a very difficult work to understand, it seemed to contain an honest and passionate view of how our concept of God and man can be illuminated by biological knowledge. I agree with parts of it, disagree with others, and don't understand some segments, but my thinking is forever changed because, like Spinoza, Teilhard points the way toward a reconciliation between religious and scientific thought. Writing of Teilhard, Julian Huxley, a distinguished evolutionary biologist, notes:

> His influence on the world's thinking is bound to be important. Through his combination of wide scientific knowledge with deep religious feeling and a rigorous

248

sense of values, he has forced theologians to view their ideas in the new perspective of evolution, and scientists to see the spiritual implications of their knowledge. He has both clarified and unified our vision of reality. In the light of that new comprehension, it is no longer possible to maintain that science and religion must operate in thought-tight compartments or concern separate sectors of life; they are both relevant to the whole of human existence. The religiously-minded can no longer turn their backs upon the natural world, or seek escape from its imperfections in a supernatural world; nor can the materialistically-minded deny importance to spiritual experience and religious feeling.

I think that scientists like Medawar, Monod, and Gould are of a generation deeply committed to keeping science totally apart from any ties to religion. Immersed in paradigm that goes back to Darwin's defender Thomas Huxley and his coinage of the word "agnostic," they are suspicious of Teilhard's Jesuit credentials and refuse his notion that to understand the phenomenon of man we must understand the whole phenomenon, the human mind, the human spirit, and human influence on the very thing being studied. But in our search for objectivity we cannot deny the obvious, all those aspects of *Homo sapiens* that go beyond the normal laboratory observations.

Teilhard's message is that "all around us, as far as the eye can see, the universe holds together, and only one way of considering it is really possible, that is, to take it as a whole, in one piece." That synthetic philosophical statement is difficult for scientists who normally proceed by analysis of phenomena into their simplest parts, which are then studied in detail. But there really is no necessary inconsistency between a science that reduces all phenomena to basic principles and a philosophy that reassembles the underlying understanding into a synthetic overview.

Before going further into Teilhard's thoughts, let's say a word about the man. Pierre was born in 1881, in Auvergne, France, the son of a small landowner. His birth, just a year before the death of Charles Darwin, places his education in that period of dreadful confrontation between biologists and theologians. Teilhard carried within himself, as did few others, the pain of that confrontation. His early education was in a Jesuit school where he specialized in geology. At eighteen he made his decision to be a religious and a scientist. In 1912 he became an ordained priest.

During his studies he had been much influenced by reading *Creative Evolution*, by Henri Bergson. And at the risk of getting into a regress, a few thoughts are in order about Bergson's work. These are necessary because Bergson's most significant philosophical book, *Creative Evolution*, hailed at its publication for its insights and liberating influence, now gathers dust in libraries and is unavailable in most bookstores. Our regress into the work of nineteenth-century philosophers need go only one step beyond Bergson to Darwin's contemporary, Herbert Spencer, the philosopher of evolution whose works provided the thesis for the modification by Bergson and the great elaboration by Teilhard de Chardin.

Spencer was a self-educated engineer, philosopher, and universal scholar. He saw philosophy as a synthesis of scientific knowledge to replace the theology of the Middle Ages. An evolutionist before Darwin's publications, he saw all of existence as an evolution from the homogeneous to the heterogeneous brought about by some unspecified force. To quote the *Encyclopaedia Britannica*: "The 'law of the multiplication of effects' due to an unknown and unknowable absolute force, is in Spencer's view the clue to the understanding of all development, cosmic as well as biological."

For all the breadth of his thoughts, Spencer, along with Thomas Huxley and Ernst Haeckel, was a proponent of agnosticism, an advocate of a philosophy free of commitment to the divine. Although these early evolutionists introduced metaphysical notions such as the will to survive, they kept insisting that they were free of metaphysics. They belonged to that generation of thinkers that had to make a sharp break with traditional Christianity in order to assert that life arose spontaneously on the earth and man descended from nonhuman primates. In so doing they became the philosophical opponents of all search for purpose in the universe. They passionately rejected teleology, the Aristotelian notion of final causes, and in so doing they rejected the possibility that the causal laws of science might themselves be imbued with purpose.

The intellectual thrust of the scientific evolutionists was not necessarily agnostic but their rhetoric was so sharp that they did not recognize their own attachment to a world of purpose. For example, if Spencer had recognized his "unknowable absolute force" as Aristotle's "unmoved mover" he would have found himself uncomfortably close to Saint Thomas's "God of reason."

In Spencer's writings the pendulum seems to have swung all the way toward materialism, agnosticism, and social Darwinism. The reply to this extreme came in the writings of Henri Bergson, Pierre Teilhard de Chardin, and Lawrence Henderson, whose work we have already commented on. There is a line of evolutionary philosophy that goes from Spencer to Bergson to Teilhard to the modern day.

As a student of biology, Bergson, who was born in 1859, the year of publication of the *Origin of Species*, was swept up in the excitement of the emerging evolutionary theory. He was an early disciple of Herbert Spencer but rebelled against the materialism and fixity in that philosopher's views. He came to explain evolution not in terms of a kind of mechanical elimination of the unfit but in terms of what he saw as the creative surge of life, the *élan vital*. He did not, as do the fundamentalists, see life in opposition to the laws of nature; rather, within the laws of nature he saw purpose, the continuous creation of novelty, both biological and intellectual. But he saw the laws of nature going beyond Democritus' atoms and Galilei's space-time to embrace the mind and spirit as part of natural law. *Creative Evolution* ended:

> Philosophy is not only the turning of the mind homeward, the coincidence of human consciousness with the

living principle whence it emanates, a contact with the creative effort: it is the study of becoming in general, it is true evolutionism and consequently the true continuation of science—provided that we understand by this word a set of truths either experienced or demonstrated, and not a certain new scholasticism that has grown up during the latter half of the nineteenth century around the physics of Galileo, as the old scholasticism grew up around Aristotle.

These ideas of Bergson motivated Teilhard de Chardin as he set off as a priest in an order governed by the old Scholasticism to become a scientist in a cohort governed by the new Scholasticism. His life was not an easy one.

He spent the war years 1914–18 as a stretcher bearer and received the Military Medal and Legion of Honor for bravery and dedication. The postwar years from 1918 to his death in 1955 were spent as paleontologist and priest, viewed with suspicion of heresy by his Order and his Church and condemned for his teleological views by the scientific community. True to himself he set down his ideas in expansive prose and true to his vow of obedience he refrained from publishing his works without official permission, which never came. On his death in 1955 friends of Teilhard's arranged for publication of his works, including *Le Phénomène Humaine*, which appeared in English in 1959 under the title *The Phenomenon of Man*.

A few months before going off to Lahaina I was in Poughkeepsie, New York, tending to some family business. When the press of everyday activities got too heavy and with a few free hours I resolved to go to Hyde Park to visit the grave of Teilhard on the grounds of St. Andrews Seminary. When I reached the town no one could direct me to St. Andrews. I wandered around and finally located an old-time native who was tending bar at a tavern. "Oh, yes," he said, "St. Andrews is now the Culinary Institute of America. Right up the road on Route Nine." The contrast between Teilhard's intellectual agony and the epicure's culinary ecstasy came rather as a shock, but the mission was pursued.

In the security office of the Culinary Institute a uniformed officer presented a key to the cemetery gate and directions to go down a back road to a rather hidden corner of the grounds. There, indeed, in neat military fashion the graves were laid out, each with the same type of tombstone, and chronologically arranged by date of death. I found Teilhard's last resting place and stood there in the summer twilight of Hyde Park.

Herbert Spencer, Henri Bergson, and Pierre Teilhard de Chardin, although worlds apart in many ways, were the philosophers of evolution. Their thinking forms a continuous strand from Spencer's evolution of matter to Bergson's evolution of life and mind to Teilhard's evolution of mind and spirit. Evolutionary doctrine, which had been the center of conflict between science and religion in Darwin's time, became in Teilhard's mind a path to understanding God. Because that God was not the deity of his Jesuit Fathers and Brothers, his life was one of constant alienation. His vows of obedience, however, earned him a spot in the cemetery at St.

Andrews, just a short distance away from what is now a leading training ground for gourmet chefs.

Teilhard de Chardin devotes most of *The Phenomenon of Man* to recounting the history of the universe. In that sense his book resembles our previous three chapters except that he writes from the scientific perspective of the 1940s. Let us look at the points of agreement. He, too, starts with the big bang:

> Then suddenly came a swarming of elementary corpuscles, both positive and negative (protons, neutrons, electrons, photons): the list increases incessantly. Then the harmonic series of simple bodies, strung out from hydrogen to uranium on the notes of the atomic scale. Next follows the immense variety of compound bodies in which the molecular weights go on increasing up to a certain critical value above which, as we shall see, we pass on to life. There is not one term in this long series but must be regarded, from sound experimental proofs, as being composed of nuclei and electrons. This fundamental discovery that all bodies owe their origin to arrangements of a single initial corpuscular type is the beacon that lights the history of the universe to our eyes. In its own way, matter has obeyed from the beginning that great law of biology to which we shall have to refer time and time again, the law of "complexification."

He passes quickly through the formation of the solar system and Earth. Then follows a lengthy discussion of the "advent of life" and an even more extended discussion of the "expansion of life," which is a review of the evolutionary history of the past 600 million years.

Up to this point Teilhard's book is scientifically conventional, a series of scenarios based on the best available experimental evidence and theoretical understanding. Two special features animate his view and distinguish it from others. First, he gives great weight to the discontinuities:

> *The origin of the universe*
> *The formation of the solar system*
> *The advent of life*
> *The birth of thought*
> *A forthcoming transition to spirit*

Second, he sees direction in the evolutionary unfolding of the universe, the direction going from matter to organized matter to life to mind to spirit. With respect to the transitions, Teilhard's view is a slow, gradual process leading up to a sudden discontinuity. The analogy he uses is that of water being heated. The temperature gradually rises, with only qualitative changes of properties. At the boiling point a discrete discontinuity takes place; the temperature can go no higher for water but steam becomes the dominant factor.

Thus some unknown primordial condition heats up to the big bang, an event so cataclysmic it destroys all evidence of its prehistory. The transition is discontinuous. The condensing matter then heats up, generating galaxies, stars, and planets. On an astrophysical time scale the transition from atom cloud to galaxy is fast, and the new system having undergone great nuclear transformation tends to lose evidence of its prehistory. After the earth has formed, a gradual series of chemical reactions takes place leading to life. Once again the transition is overwhelming. Available carbon, hydrogen, nitrogen, oxygen, phosphorus, and sulfur are gobbled up as a layer of living material surrounds the planet.

Then Teilhard moves on to the next transition, the rise of consciousness. After providing the setting, he notes the slow three-billion-year evolution of the animals and the entire later evolutionary scheme falls into place if one focuses on the development of the nervous system. He asserts that the arrangement of animal species based on the development of a central nervous system corresponds to the classification of systematic biology. He derives from this a direction to evolution. He writes: "Among the infinite modalities in which the complication of life is dispersed, the differentiation of nervous tissue stands out, as theory would lead us to expect, as a significant transformation. *It provides a direction; and therefore it proves that evolution has a direction.*"

At the core of *The Phenomenon of Man* lies "The Expansion of Life," or the elaboration of the tree of life. It is Teilhard's argument, expressed in the biology of his day, that evolution moves from life to thought. In presenting his perspective I will rephrase it in accordance with the biology of today. This is a risky business, for rewriting the ideas of an admittedly difficult philosophical work is fraught with the danger of transmogrifying the author's thought. Hence I will not attribute the following to Teilhard de Chardin. I will merely state that it is a parallel exposition of the transition from life to thought, and hope it is true to the spirit of the original.

In the period following the origin of life, early evolution must first have given rise to the procaryotes. The early cells were either photosynthetic, capturing solar energy, or lived off the products of photosynthesizers. For the first billion years or so, bacteria and blue-green algae were probably the chief inhabitants of the seas.

The procaryotes were then followed by the eucaryotes, cells of much greater sophistication and facility for using the genetic information contained in DNA. The eucaryotes have a paired chromosome structure, so that each genetic element, each gene, occurs twice in the cell. Mutations that are not immediately beneficial can be stored because the paired gene can continue the work of the cell. The rise of the eucaryotes made possible a much more efficient evolution. It is easier to reward genetic novelty in the informationally redundant cells of eucaryotes.

During this period of the rise of the eucaryotes three strategic mechanisms must have developed: multicellularity, movement, and the eating of other organisms. The first could have begun from a simple stickiness of cell surfaces allowing clusters of genetically similar cells to spend their lives in close association. Multicellularity has one great advantage: it allows specialization by the proliferation of cell types with different functions. In other words, multicellularity is one way to build complexity into organisms.

Since all eucaryotes have a sexual cycle characterized by meiosis, which divides chromosome pairs into two sets, and fertilization, which recombines chromosomes from different cells, it follows that each eucaryotic organism must start out as a single cell with paired chromosomes. Thus a multicellular organism with different cell types displays a developmental process by which a single cell gives rise by successive divisions to an entire organism. This facility for developmental process also represents a new biological potential, which arose somewhere in the Archeozoic Era.

Motility is the ability to carry out mechanical motion and it developed among flagellated bacteria, ciliated protozoa and specialized motile cells in simple multicellular organisms. Motility confers an enormous advantage to organisms, allowing them to seek food and favorable environments and to avoid unfavorable ones. Motility also allows organisms to change environments by moving objects around.

A current theory of endosymbiosis suggests that most cellular organelles of eucaryotes developed first as procaryotes that began to live inside the eucaryotic cell in a symbiotic relationship. The procaryote gradually lost the ability to exist independently and became an organelle. Thus mitochondria are supposed to have developed from aerobic bacteria, chloroplasts are supposed to have developed from blue-green algae, and ciliary basal bodies are assumed to have developed from motile bacteria. If this theory turns out to be verified, it will more closely interrelate the evolutionary histories of procaryotes and eucaryotes.

With motility, predation, or catching live food, became possible, since the predator was free to seek out
prey and then consume it. For to both predator and
prey the ability to move is an important feature. Predation developed among the unicellular protozoa, who
learned to eat bacteria, fungi, and other protozoa. Among
the metazoans, or multicellular forms, predation developed with the primitive organisms resembling today's
hydras, creatures often seen with a magnifying glass in
pond water samples.

The hydras are members of the phylum *Coelenterata*,
which is the most primitive group of organisms to show
a tissue grade of construction. It includes jellyfish,
corals, and a wide variety of radially symmetrical marine
organisms. Of special interest to us at the moment, the
coelenterates are the lowest animals to possess a nervous
system.

Sometime in the distant past, during the differentiation of cells, the nerve cell came into being. It is generally a very elongated cell that has at least two points
of contact with other nerve cells, muscle cells, or sensory
cells. Nerves take in informational signals at receptors,
conduct them electrically along the wirelike elongated
sections, and transmit the information to neighboring
cells at effector sites. On the output side, nerves transmit
information to active loci such as muscle cells causing
them to contract or inhibiting that contraction. With the
existence of a nerve network, all parts of an animal
rapidly communicate with all other parts and a new
level of activity is possible. The evolution of the nerve
cell was an absolute necessity for the occurrence of

higher animal life. It seems to have taken between one and two billion years of evolutionary activity to produce a functional neuron. Once developed, the mode of signal communication seems similar across the phyla. The appearance of nerve cells is one of those occurrences that changed the world in a major way.

The radially symmetrical coelenterate animals, like hydra and jellyfish, that originally developed in the sea all appear to have a diffuse nervous system, a net of cells throughout the entire animal body with no nerve bundles and no region of central control. The sensory cells of these animals are widely distributed.

The next major step in animal evolution was the appearance of bilateral symmetry, a plan of construction that involves a similar right and left side. The flatworms are its most primitive example. The diffuse nervous system is replaced by more central structures, bundles of nerves called ganglia. There often emerges a cerebral ganglion at the head end. There is a general tendency seen in animal evolution for sensory function such as vision and perception of chemicals to become centralized in the head region, as well as for the mouth to be associated with this part of the body. This moving of neural function to the head is called cephalization by Teilhard.

Following the evolution of bilateral symmetry, animals diverge into two major branches, the chordates leading to the vertebrates, and the invertebrates including the annelid worms and the arthropods (crabs, insects, spiders, centipedes, etc.). The chordates develop in the direction of internal skeletons, bony structures that leave fossil remains. The invertebrates move toward shells and outer skeletons, which also produce fossil remains. Most major phyla have representatives as early as 500 million years ago and the evolution that paleontologists study is the radiation and development of these phyla.

In this section there is an emphasis on animals rather than on plants because the thrust of Teilhard's argument is toward consciousness and man, both within the world of animals. He sums up with a poetic view of the tree of life:

"And, to end with, the whole assemblage, animal and vegetable, forming by association one giant biota, is rooted perhaps like a simple stem in some verticil [whirl] steeped in the depths of the mega-molecular [we would say macromolecular] world."

In looking at the whole of animal life, Teilhard sees beyond the tendency for cephalization the rise of cerebralization, the formation of a brain. He sees this tendency in all higher animal forms. He then says: "We began by saying that, among living creatures, the brain was the sign and measure of consciousness. We have now added that, among living creatures, the brain is continually perfecting itself with time. . . ."

In the *Phenomenon of Man* the neuroanatomy and physiology are discussed in some detail. Of course, this field of biology has experienced enormous progress since Teilhard set down his words in 1940. What persists is the idea that evolution led from a diffuse neural net (hydra) to bundles of control nerves called ganglia (flatworms) to a nerve-rich head region (all higher phyla). From the reptiles to the mammals there is the continuous growth in size and complexity of the brain. This tendency is maximized in the primates.

Next in *The Phenomenon of Man* comes "The Rise of Consciousness" and "The Birth of Thought." The main sweep of these sections is the threefold idea that animal evolution is accompanied by cerebralization, or brain formation; brain function is associated with consciousness; and consciousness leads to thought. Thus for Teilhard, brain, consciousness, thought are our biological heritage arising from the laws of physics and organic life and pointing onward to the world of the spirit. They are somehow inherent in the big bang, part of an unfolding cosmic plan, not deterministic in detail but broadly constrained along the main pathway.

Teilhard accepts consciousness as a necessary feature of higher animal life. He believes it is obvious that animals are aware of their environment, and that this awareness is both related to brain function and increases in intensity with larger brain size. This consciousness reaches its highest degree in the mammals. The behavior of mammals is "so supple, so unexpected, exhibits such exuberance of life and curiosity."

Consciousness is to Teilhard the "within of organisms." Physiology, biochemistry, and reductionist approaches are to him the without of organisms. He argues that we cannot understand man or the living world without seeing the within of things as well as the without. He writes as a scientist explaining why this broader view is necessary. Having established a view of consciousness, Teilhard moves to "The Birth of Thought."

Consciousness, which for Teilhard is a property of all animals with nerve cells, develops intensively in the mammalian line as an accompaniment of the growth and complexification of the brain. This is especially seen along the primate line of descent, where development of the hands and full binocular vision accompany brain development.

At some time late in the evolution of primates an enormous transformation occurs, the evolution from consciousness to reflection. For the flavor of Teilhard's assessment of the profundity of this event, let's turn to his own words:

> From our experimental point of view, reflection is, as the word indicates, the power acquired by a consciousness to turn in upon itself, to take possession of itself *as of an object* endowed with its own particular consistence and value: no longer merely to know, but to know oneself; no longer merely to know, but to know that one knows. By this individualisation of himself in the depths of himself, the living element, which heretofore had been spread out and divided over a diffuse circle of perceptions and activities, was constituted for the first time as a *centre* in the form of a point at which all the impressions and experiences knit themselves together and fuse into a unity that is conscious of its own organisation.
>
> Now the consequences of such a transformation are immense, visible as clearly in nature as any of the facts recorded by physics or astronomy. The being who is the object of his own reflection, in consequence of that very doubling back upon himself, becomes in a flash able to raise himself into a new sphere. In reality, another world is born. Abstraction, logic, reasoned choice and inventions, mathematics, art, calculation of space and time, anxieties

and dreams of love—all these activities of *inner life* are nothing else than the effervescence of the newly-formed centre as it explodes onto itself.

We are now at one of the real keys to the thought of Pierre Teilhard de Chardin. The point is that humans and to some extent other higher primates are radically different from all other animals because of reflective thought. We do not know how and exactly when this property emerged, but we know that once it exists it changes the world in a cataclysmic way. Reflective thought is as radical a transformation as life, and its existence will alter the planet just as profoundly as life altered the nonliving planet. Using computer terminology, the distance between us and the animals is not a hardware distinction; rather, a revolution in software occurred that totally altered the species and the planet.

Just as life spread out to become the biosphere, so thought spreads out to become the noosphere, the interacting realm of thought that is society, culture, humanity.

It seems strange to think that there is or ever was anything radical in Teilhard's notion that humans are so different from other animals that they alter the world in ways totally unforeseen from a knowledge of biology. Such a result was so apparent to pre-Darwinians that it needed no discussion. The post-Darwinian biologists, in an effort to prove a point about the descent of man, ignored how very, very different humans are from all other life. History is in no way predictable from biology; it involves a species whose reflective thought changes all the rules. Most evolutionists closed their eyes to the obvious properties of *Homo sapiens* and sociobiologists have made a deliberate effort to ignore it. But the most radical part of Teilhard's thinking is truly an announcement of the obvious.

We are now in the age of the deployment of the noosphere, the radical change in the planet caused by the spread of the mind of man altering the planet.

At present we leave Teilhard's vision looking forward to the emergence of spirit to take hold after the noosphere. He departs the realm of science to enter the realm of even more speculative thought. For to Teilhard, it was personally important to complete the journey from evolution to the God of faith, regardless of the intellectual difficulties of that position. If we part company at this point, it is with profound thanks to this savant for having illuminated who we are and where we have come from.

CHAPTER 17

Mind and Matter

The biology of man brings us to some difficult philosophical problems of the relation of mind and matter, mind and body, and mind and brain. If, following Teilhard, we define consciousness in terms of sensing the environment and responding to those sensations, then the concept can be removed from the philosophical arena. Focusing first on consciousness in those animals with sensory cells and neurons, we then would be tempted to extend the property down the phylogenetic tree to motile bacteria that are able to sense the rate of change of concentration of certain chemicals in their environment and swim toward food and away from poisons. Sensing the environment and responding is also a characteristic of plants, with their various tropisms, slow growth-responses to environmental signals. Consciousness in this sense seems almost coexistent with life, although it took a quantum leap forward with the evolution of the neuron.

Reflective thought is a different matter; it involves consciousness of being conscious, knowing that we know. The capacity for reflective thought is a description of *mind* in the philosophical sense; it entered the world with the higher primates and reached its peak along the hominid line of evolution. Focusing on mind in formulating the natural sciences was preeminent in the 1600s, receded in the 1700s and 1800s, and made a remarkable comeback in the 1900s. It's going to be necessary to follow a bit of that story to better understand current perspectives.

René Descartes, one of the founders of modern philosophy, made a sharp distinction between mind and body. He envisioned a human being as a union between a purely mechanical body and a mind or soul existing outside the laws of physics. Reflective thought was clearly in the province of the mind for Descartes, although he never solved the problem of how the non-material mind and the material body can interact with each other, since mind and body are such inherently different substances. For Descartes, God's creation of man was the attachment of mind to an animal body. These views persisted for a long time in the scientific community and made possible the study of physics independent of any mentalist notions. Since Descartes denied that animals had minds, his views facilitated a purely materialistic biology.

Benedict Spinoza was highly critical of Descartes's

dualist views because he questioned how a nonphysical mind could interact with a body and how a transcendent God could interact with the world. Spinoza, in clear contrast to Descartes, regarded mind and body as complementary aspects of the same underlying substance. Because Descartes had divorced mind and matter, it was possible for Isaac Newton in 1690 to ignore the mind and formulate physics in terms of an absolute space and absolute time that were independent of the observer.

Both Descartes's and Spinoza's views stand in opposition to those of the materialists, who maintain that all that exists in matter and mind is an epiphenomenon, a curious sort of illusion of very complex material systems. Thus the early Greek atomist Democritus said that all reality consists of atoms and a void. This view has been the perspective of many nineteenth- and twentieth-century biologists who, observing how successfully classical physics had been formulated with only material constructs, wanted to formulate biology on the same basis. It is an approach that has many adherents today. A most radical statement of this view was set forth by the mid-nineteenth-century physiologist Emil Du Bois-Reymond. He asserted: "Nevertheless, if our methods only were sufficient, an analytical mechanics of the general life process would be possible. This conviction rests on the insight . . . that all changes in the material world . . . reduce to motions. Therefore even the life process cannot be anything but motions. . . . This reduction would indeed initiate an analytical mechanics of those processes. One sees therefore that if the difficulty of analysis did not exceed our ability, analytical mechanics fundamentally would reach even to the problem of freedom of the will."

Opposed to the materialist doctrine is the position of idealism best known in the works of George Berkeley (1685–1753). He asserts that only mind exists and all common shared experiences as well as physical objects are the result of those ideas existing in the mind of God. It is the only philosophy I know of that is best expressed by two limericks written by English students, so we should proceed to that unusual genre of philosophical writing.

> There was a young man who said, "God,
> to you it must seem very odd
>   that a tree as a tree
>   simply ceases to be
> when there's no one about in the quad."

God answers:

> "Young man, your astonishment's odd;
> I'm always about in the quad
>   and that's why the tree
>   never ceases to be
> as observed by, yours faithfully, God."

During the late 1800s, most biologists were materialists in the Democritean tradition. This outlook gave them a protected agnostic position to pursue their evolutionary studies. Most physicists were materialists in the tradition of Pierre-Simon de Laplace (1749–1827).

When Laplace presented his book on celestial mechanics to Napoleon, the ruler remarked that he saw no mention of God. The astrophysicist replied, "Sire, I have no need of that hypothesis."

In the 1890s and early 1900s, Vienna became the center of positivism, a system of philosophy based solely on the positive data of sense experience. The followers of that view reject speculations about ultimate origins or underlying reality. Positivist philosophy is presently out of fashion, although at one time under the leadership of Ernst Mach it exerted a powerful influence.

What has happened to the twentieth-century views of physicists and biologists is rather strange. Biologists, who under the banner of vitalism once postulated a privileged role for life and the human mind in nature's hierarchy, have been moving steadily toward the materialism that characterized nineteenth-century physics. At the same time, twentieth-century physicists, faced with compelling experimental evidence, have been moving away from mechanical models of the universe to a view that sees the mind as playing an integral role in all observed physical events.

The study of life at all levels, from social to molecular behavior, has in modern times relied on reductionism as the chief explanatory concept. This approach to knowledge tries to comprehend one level of scientific phenomena in terms of concepts at a lower and presumably more fundamental level. In chemistry, large-scale reactions are accounted for by examining the behavior of molecules. Similarly, physiologists study the activity of living cells in terms of processes carried out by organelles and other subcellular entities. And in geology, the formations and properties of minerals are described using the features of the constituent crystals. The essence of these cases lies in seeking explanation in underlying structures and activities.

Reductionism at the mental level is exemplified by Carl Sagan's book *The Dragons of Eden*. He writes: "My fundamental premise about the brain is that its workings—what we sometimes call 'mind'—are a consequence of its anatomy and physiology and nothing more." As a further demonstration of this trend of thought, we note that his glossary does not contain the words "mind," "consciousness," "perception," "awareness," or "thought," but rather deals with entries such as "synapse," "lobotomy," "proteins," and "electrodes."

Attempts to reduce human behavior to its biological basis have a long history, beginning with the early Darwinians and their contemporaries working in physiological psychology. Before the nineteenth century, the mind-body duality, which was central to Descartes's philosophy, had tended to place the human mind outside the domain of biology. Then the stress that the evolutionists placed on our "apeness" made us subject to biological study by methods appropriate to nonhuman primates and, by extension, to other animals. The Pavlovian school of action-reaction psychology reinforced that theme, and it became a cornerstone of many behavioral theories. While no general agreement has emerged among psychologists as to how far reductionism should be carried, all will concede that our actions have hormonal, neurological, and physiological components.

Although Sagan's premise lies within a general tradition in psychology, it is radical in aiming at *complete* explanation in terms of the underlying level. This goal I take to be the thrust of his phrase "and nothing more."

While some psychologists were attempting to reduce their science to biology, other life scientists were also looking for more basic levels of explanation. Their outlook can be seen in the writings of a popular spokesman of molecular biology, Francis Crick. In his book *Of Molecules and Men*, a contemporary attack on vitalism —the doctrine that biology needs to be explained in terms of life forces lying outside the domain of physics— Crick states: "The ultimate aim of the modern movement in biology is in fact to explain *all* biology in terms of physics and chemistry." By physics and chemistry he refers to the atomic level, where our knowledge is secure. By use of the italicized *all*, he expresses the position of radical reductionism that has been the dominant viewpoint among an entire generation of biochemists and molecular biologists.

If we now combine psychological and biological reductionism and assume they overlap, we end up with a sequence of explanations going from mind to anatomy and physiology, to cell physiology, to molecular biology, to atomic physics. All knowledge is assumed to rest on a firm bedrock of understanding: the laws of quantum mechanics. Within the context, psychology becomes a branch of physics, a result that may cause some unease among both groups of professionals.

This attempt to explain everything about human beings in terms of the first principles of physical science is not a new idea and had reached a definitive position in the views of the mid-nineteenth-century European physiologists. There is a certain hubris in this position that was picked up by Thomas Huxley and his colleagues in their defense of Darwinism and, even today, echoes in the theories of reductionists who would move from the mind to the first principles of atomic physics. It is most clearly seen, at present, in the writings of sociobiologists, whose arguments animate the contemporary intellectual scene. In any case, Du Bois-Reymond's earliest views stated above are consistent with those of the modern radical reductionists, except that quantum mechanics has now replaced Newtonian mechanics as the underlying discipline.

During the period in which psychologists and biologists were steadily moving toward reducing their disciplines to the physical sciences, they were largely unaware of perspectives emerging from physics that cast an entirely new light on their understanding. Toward the close of the last century, physics presented a very ordered picture of the world, in which events unfolded in characteristic, regular ways, following Newton's equations in mechanics and Maxwell's equations in electricity. The latter make it possible to derive all the observed phenomena of electricity and magnetism, including electromagnetic waves, from a small number of basic equations. These processes moved inexorably, independent of the scientist, who was simply a spectator. Many physicists considered their subject essentially complete.

Starting with the introduction of the theory of special relativity by Albert Einstein in 1905, this neat picture was unceremoniously upset. The new theory postulated that observers in different systems moving with respect to each other would perceive the world differently. The observer thus became involved in establishing physical reality. The scientist was losing the spectator's role and once again becoming an active participant in the system under study.

With the development of quantum mechanics, the role of the observer became even more central, an essential component in defining an event. The mind of the observer emerged as a necessary element in the structure of the theory. The implications of the developing paradigm greatly surprised early quantum physicists and led them to study epistemology and the philosophy of science. Never before in scientific history had all of the leading contributors produced books and papers expounding the philosophical and humanistic meaning of their results.

Werner Heisenberg, one of the founders of the new physics, became deeply involved in the issues of philosophy and humanism. In *Philosophical Problems of Quantum Physics*, he wrote of physicists having to renounce thoughts of an objective time scale common to all observers, and of events in time and space that are independent of our ability to observe them. Heisenberg stressed that the laws of nature no longer dealt with elementary particles, but with our knowledge of these particles—that is, *with the contents of our minds*. Erwin

Schrödinger, the man who formulated the fundamental equation of quantum mechanics, wrote an extraordinary little book in 1958 called *Mind and Matter*. In this series of essays, he moved from the results of the new physics to a rather mystical view of the universe that he identified with the "perennial philosophy" of Aldous Huxley. Schrödinger was the first of the quantum theoreticians to express sympathy with the Upanishads and Eastern philosophical thought. A growing body of literature now embodies this perspective.

One problem faced by quantum theorists can best be see in the famous paradox "Who killed Schrödinger's cat?" In a hypothetical formulation, a kitten is put in a closed box with a jar of poison and a trip-hammer poised to smash the jar. The hammer is activated by a counter that records random events, such as radioactive decay. The experiment lasts just long enough for there to be a probability of one-half that the hammer will be released. Quantum mechanics represents the system mathematically by the sum of a live-cat and a dead-cat wave function, each with a probability of one-half. The question is whether the act of looking (the measurement) kills or saves the cat, since before the experimenter looks in the box, both solutions are equally likely.

This whimsical example reflects a deep conceptual difficulty. In more formal terms, a complex system can be described only by using a probability distribution that relates the possible outcomes of an experiment. In order to decide among the various alternatives, a measurement is required. This measurement is what constitutes an event, as distinguished from the probability, which is a mathematical abstraction. However, the only simple and consistent description physicists were able to assign to a measurement involved an observer's becoming aware of the result. Thus the physical event and the content of the human mind were inseparable. This linkage forced many researchers seriously to consider consciousness or human thought as an integral part of the structure of physics. Such interpretations moved science toward the *idealist* as contrasted with the *realist* conception of philosophy.

The views of a large number of contemporary physical scientists are summed up in the essay "Remarks on the Mind-Body Question" written by Nobel laureate Eugene Wigner. Wigner begins by pointing out that most physical scientists have returned to the recognition that thought—meaning the mind—is primary. He goes on to state: "It was not possible to formulate the laws of quantum mechanics in a fully consistent way without reference to the consciousness." And he concludes by noting how remarkable it is that the scientific study of the world led to the content of consciousness as an ultimate reality.

A further development in yet another field of physics reinforces Wigner's viewpoint. The introduction of information theory and its application to thermodynamics has led to the conclusion that entropy, a basic concept of that science, is a measure of the observer's ignorance of the atomic details of a system. When we measure the pressure, volume, and temperature of an object, we have a residual lack of knowledge of the exact position and velocity of the component atoms and molecules. The numerical value of the amount of information we are missing is proportional to the entropy. In earlier thermodynamics, entropy had represented, in an engineering sense, the energy of the system unavailable to perform external work. In the modern view, the human mind enters once again, and entropy relates not just to the state of the system but to knowledge of that state.

The founders of modern atomic theory did not start out to impose a "mentalist" picture on the world. Rather, they began with the opposite point of view and were forced to the present-day position in order to explain experimental results.

We are now able to integrate perspectives of psychology, biology, and physics. First, it is asserted that the human mind, including consciousness and reflective thought, can be explained by activities of the central nervous system, which, in turn, can be reduced to the biological structure and function of that physiological system. Second, biological phenomena at all levels can be totally understood in terms of atomic physics, that is, through the action and interaction of the component atoms of carbon, nitrogen, oxygen, and so forth. Third and last, atomic physics, which is now understood most fully by means of quantum mechanics, must be formulated with the mind as a primitive component of the system.

We have thus, in separate steps, gone around an epistemological circle—from the mind to the mind. The results of this chain of reasoning will probably lend more aid and comfort to Eastern mystics than to neurophysiologists and molecular biologists; nevertheless, the closed loop follows from a straightforward combination of the explanatory processes of recognized experts in the three separate sciences. Since individuals seldom work with more than one of these paradigms, the general problem has received little attention.

If we reject this epistemological circularity, we are left with two opposing camps: a physics with a claim to completeness because it describes all of nature, and a psychology that is all-embracing because it deals with the mind, our only source of knowledge of the world. Given the problems in both of these views, it is perhaps well to return to the circle and give it more sympathetic consideration. If it deprives us of firm absolutes, at least it encompasses the mind-body problem and provides a framework within which individual disciplines can communicate.

The strictly reductionist approach to human behavior so characteristic of sociobiology also runs into trouble on more narrowly biological grounds. For it includes a postulate of continuity in evolution from early mammals to man, which implies that the mind, or reflective thought, was not a radical departure. Such an assumption is questionable when one considers the dramatic effects on the planet that have resulted from the presence of *Homo sapiens*.

The encoding of information in genetic molecules introduced the possibility of profound disturbances in the deterministic laws that governed the universe. Before the coming of genetic life, for example, fluctuations in temperature or noise were averaged out, giving rise to precise laws of planetary evolution. Afterward, however, a single molecular event at the level of thermal noise could lead to macroscopic consequences. For if the event were a mutation in a self-replicating system, then the entire course of biological evolution could be altered. A single molecular event could kill a whale by inducing a cancer or destroy an ecosystem by generating a virulent virus that attacks a key species in that system. The origin of coding does not abrogate the underlying laws of physics, but it adds a new feature: large-scale consequences of molecular events. This change in the rules makes evolutionary history incompletely determinate and so constitutes a clear-cut discontinuity.

The fact that evolution is not completely determinate does not mean that it is totally random. Beyond the laws of molecular physics there are information and strategy relations and considerations of population biology and energetic ecology. These higher order relations structure but do not totally confine the unfolding of biological history.

A number of contemporary biologists and psychologists believe that the origin of reflective thought that occurred during primate evolution is a discontinuity that has changed the rules. Again, the new situation does not abrogate the underlying biological laws, but it adds a feature that necessitates novel ways of thinking about the problem. The evolutionary biologist Lawrence B. Slobodkin has identified the new feature as an introspective self-image, which seems the same as Teilhard's reflective thought. This property, he asserts, alters the response to evolutionary problems and makes it impossible to assign major historical events to causes inherent in biological evolutionary laws. Slobodkin is claiming as a biologist that the rules have changed, and man cannot be understood by laws applicable to other mammals whose brains have a very similar physiology. The rules have changed twice: once with encoding of genetic information in macromolecules and again with the appearance of thought.

The emergent features of man have, in one form or another, been discussed by numerous anthropologists, psychologists, and biologists. It is part of the empirical data that cannot be shelved just to preserve reductionist purity. The discontinuity needs to be thoroughly studied and evaluated, but first it needs to be recognized. Primates are different from other animals, and human beings are very different from other primates.

We now understand the troublesome features in a forceful commitment to uncritical reductionism as a solution to the problem of mind. We have discussed the weaknesses of that position. In addition to being weak, it is dangerous, since the way we respond to our fellow humans is dependent on the way we conceptualize them in our theoretical formulations. If we envision our fellows solely as animals or machines, we drain our interactions of humanistic richness. If we seek our behavioral norms in the study of animal societies, we ignore those uniquely human features that so enrich our lives. Radical reductionism offers very little in the area of moral imperatives. Further, it presents the wrong glossary of terms for a humanistic pursuit.

The scientific community has made notable progress in understanding the brain, and there is a great sense of excitement about the developing neurosciences. Nevertheless, we should be reluctant to let that élan generate statements that lock us into philosophical positions that impoverish our humanity by denying the most intriguing aspect of our species. To underrate the significance of the appearance and character of reflective thought is a high price to pay in order to honor the liberation of science from theology by our reductionist predecessors several generations back. The human psyche is part of the observed data of science. We can retain it and still be good empirical biologists and psychologists.

What emerges from all this is the return of "mind" to all areas of scientific thought. This is good news from the point of view of all varieties of natural theology. For a universe where mind is a fundamental part of reality more easily makes contact with the mind of god than does a mindless world.

CHAPTER 18

An Abode of Life

As you've probably guessed by now, tucked in my boxes of books in the stowage underneath the portside bunk is a copy of *Walden, or, Life in the Woods*, by Henry David Thoreau. That volume came out this afternoon for a rereading of Thoreau's speculations about beings in distant parts of the universe. He dreams about life in the Pleiades or behind Cassiopeia's Chair. He muses about "different beings in the various mansions of the universe" who are contemplating the same star he is viewing. He meditates about a cosmic triangle with a distant star at one vertex, himself at the second, and some remote thinking being at the third. Intelligent life in the universe was not a strange thought on the shores of Walden Pond.

With Thoreau's words to feed the mind and Burger King's takeout to feed the body, we've walked from Lahaina along the coast of Launiupoko to sit on the beach and watch the sunset. At the risk of sounding like the visitor's bureau, let's affirm that sunsets from the western shores of Hawaiian Islands are spectacular. Tonight's is no exception. A few minutes after the sun is down, a pink-streaked afterglow lights up the sky and slowly fades into darkness. After it is fully dark and the myriad stars and galaxies come into view, we stay to give some attention to the thoughts of the sage of Walden. In the darkness and clear air of Launiupoko, the night sky seems alive with tiny lights on a field of absolute blackness.

The question of the moment is where else in the universe is reflective thought to be found. I recall reading Loren Eiseley on the terrible loneliness of looking out and thinking that perhaps there is no one else, the awesome responsibility of the universe is all ours, and we may fail. However, thought has shifted on that issue and the present consensus is that we are one among many, perhaps very many. In any case, enough is now known to pose the question in more precise ways.

First, a consideration of energetics and chemical structure suggests that a favorable home for life would almost certainly have to be on a planet orbiting a star formed from the debris of previous stellar explosions. The debris requirement is necessary for the condensing solar system to have enough atoms other than hydrogen and helium. The planetary requirement is imposed by the necessity of being an intermediate system between an energy source and an energy sink.

At present there is no way of knowing for sure about planetary systems aside from our own. However, the study of the angular momentum of condensing stellar systems suggests the likelihood of planetary systems around many if not most stars. The requirement for a solar system made from the debris of a previous stellar explosion seems easily met in a 15-billion-year-old universe since many star types have life spans quite short in comparison to the age of the universe.

To be an abode of life it is not only necessary to be a planet, but there is a further requirement: to be the right distance from the right kind of star. Stars are classified by temperature as O, B, A, F, G, K, M (Oh, be a fine girl, kiss me). The O stars are at 30,000 degrees absolute, B stars are between 11,000° and 30,000°, A stars 7,200° to 11,000°, F stars 6,000° to 7,200°, G stars 5,200° to 6,000°, K stars, 3,500° to 5,200° and M stars below 3,500°.

A planet around an O star would be blasted by such intense ultraviolet and X radiation that stable chemicals could not form and persist. In addition, these objects radiating energy six hundred times as fast as the sun quickly burn up and do not allow time for planetary life to develop. M stars, on the other hand, radiate almost entirely in the infrared and lack enough visible light to drive the photochemistry necessary for life processes.

Our sun is a G star, with most of the energy as the photochemically active visible light optimal for any kind of photosynthesis. On the basis of radiation type, F, G, and K stars could have living planets and some possibility exists for A stars. O, B, and M star types appear to be definitely ruled out for living solar systems.

A planet needs also to be the proper distance from

the right kind of star. Mercury, which is four-tenths as far from the sun as earth, is too hot for stable organic components. Saturn, which is ten times as far from the sun as earth, has a temperature near that of liquid nitrogen. In that cold, reactions are far too slow for life to evolve.

Another feature is required for an abode of life. A certain mathematical relation must hold involving the radius, mass, and solar flux in order for the planet to have and to hold an atmosphere. As I sit on the beach writing by the light of a Coleman lantern, it seems out of place to work out the details of that mathematical relation, but trust me, it can be done. We've already discussed what's needed to have an atmosphere. The gravitational grip must just balance the thermal escaping tendency. A complex set of requirements is beginning to emerge that includes star type, distance from star, and size and density of the planet. The conditions are restrictive but they do not make the earth unique.

Two other features would seem of importance to guarantee any life we know or can at present envision. The planet must be wet, not necessarily as wet as the earth, but some free water must exist. Here free water is distinguished from the water of hydration bound up in crystalline aggregates, such as in Portland cement.

The other necessary feature for continuous life is a dynamic geologically active planet that undergoes mineral recycling so as to regenerate the elements necessary for life. On earth this dynamism comes from the convection of the magma, the basal lithosphere. The energy to drive this convection comes from radioactive decay within the interior and from gravitational condensation. The requirement for an active planet would lie in its atomic composition. Sufficient radioactive material is needed, which is equivalent to a need for high atomic weight nuclei. It may be necessary to be a planet of a third-generation star in order to have enough stored nuclear energy to be tectonically active.

At this point I turn off the lantern and dark adapt for a while. The moon is not yet out, it is a cloudless night, and the stars shine forth in sharp contrast to the night sky. I do not think that we are alone. One surmises that amid all the second- and third-generation A, F, G, and K stars out there, there are many with the right-size planets and appropriate conditions lying in the huge spherical shell surrounding the centers of those solar systems.

Among those planets, many must have water, since hydrogen and oxygen are common elements in the nuclear chemistry of the stars. Likewise, many second- and third-generation planets must have sufficient radioactivity generated in stellar fusion reactions.

It seems extremely improbable that life is unique to us; more likely it permeates the universe and flourishes in those niches where the conditions are favorable. The fourth law of thermodynamics guarantees the organization of planetary surfaces. The radiation of A, F, G, and K stars guarantees photochemical processes leading to chemical organization. The temperatures of planets is stabilized by the fourth-power radiation law. Stellar nuclear fusion reactions produce the right range of elements. When the setting is right, the laws of nature inexorably work their way and planets spring to life, becoming biotic, then noosphere-producing, or noetic, and ever reaching for something more.

There is another sense in which we are not alone. The awesome cosmic intelligence that surrounds us is also within us. The universality of the laws of nature is at least one way in which we are part of the world mind. Even if transcedence is beyond our grasp, the immanence of god is awfully impressive all by itself. Lying on the beach at Launiupoko and looking up at the stars, one feels the emotions that religious experiences are made of.

CHAPTER 19

Pantheism and Design

In the Campo de' Fiori (Field of Flowers) in Rome is a large statue of Giordano Bruno. Near the statue drug dealers sell heroin and other controlled substances. On February 17, 1600, the piazza was illuminated by a fire fueled in part by the same Giordano Bruno, condemned to death for heresy. The light of that fire has been reflected in several facets of European and Western intellectual history.

It is difficult to discern from our present perspective which heresy Bruno paid for. He was a complex individual and combined medieval superstition with modern rationalism. He was a magus, a magician in the sense of trying to find methods to influence the world or to forecast coming events. He was also a believer in the immanence of God, the belief that God stood within nature rather than standing over nature in some transcendent fashion. That belief in itself would in 1600 have been ground enough for his heresy conviction.

Bruno's contemporary, René Descartes, also saw the powerful influence of natural law in determining the unfolding of events. He, however, withheld from denying transcendence and thus kept his shaky peace with established authority. By sharply separating mind and body, Descartes could pursue physics independently of theology and leave such questions to the domain of the mind.

In the mid-to-late 1600s Spinoza set forth a philosophy that has come to be known as pantheism. That word has two meanings and in connection with the philosophy of Spinoza it refers to the belief that god is not a personality but all the laws, forces, substances, and manifestations of the universe; it is the doctrine of an immanent god. There is nothing unusual or extreme about pantheism as so defined. It is the everyday working faith of many scientists and humanists. Some might not want to admit it or might be a bit embarrassed to discuss it, but it is one of the major religious philosophies of our time.

For Spinoza the chief purpose of philosophy was ethics, how an individual should live. To answer this question required a physics and a metaphysics answering the question: What is the universe like? For knowing how to act must depend on what kind of world we live in. Happiness for him became the "recognition of essences involved in and implicated in the existence of things." Let's try to reword that philosophical jargon. Ethics consists in attempting to live according to the divine plan. That majestic protocol is written in nature because the divine and the everyday operations of the world are one and the same. The study of nature is the beginning of ethics, for the search for knowledge is the search for the understanding of god, since god and nature are the same. Therefore science, scholarship, all honest inquiry, is a religious act, the search for the cosmic plan. The altar of one's religion can be a lab bench, a library, or a computer if the inquiry has ethical purpose. The eternal light can be a Bunsen burner. Scholar Richard McKeon has summed up this aspect of Spinoza's thought: "Good action and intelligent action are impossible without enough understanding of God and of bodies and of the mind to make clear what is implicated in the existence of anything and in the continuance of anything, idea or essence, through change."

In somewhat more passionate prose than Spinoza would have approved of, we note that the supreme divine gift is thought, reason, and understanding. Pantheistic ethics asks us to use that gift to understand the universe in which the gift came to be so as to better our responses. Pantheistic religion asks us to love that universe. And Benedict Spinoza stood on the brink of a profound new understanding of the world, the physics of Isaac Newton, whose *Principia* appeared in print just a few years after Spinoza's death. The new mechanics was enormously powerful because it enabled scientists to start with a small number of postulates and predict in great detail the motions of the solar system.

The insights of Bruno and Spinoza and the power of Newtonian mechanics led to a popular approach to theology that flourished from 1690 to 1800. Termed physicotheology, this philosophical approach reasoned from the perfection of nature's laws to the existence, beneficence, and omnipotence of the creator. The general outlook goes back to Aristotle and the unmoved mover, but in the post-Newtonian explosion of scientific knowledge, the approach took on a new poetic glow of certainty. Alexander Pope is perhaps the best known of these Newtonian writers.

A school of English poets expanded the theme of moving from the laws of physics to God. In 1718 Matthew Prior wrote:

> From nature's constant or eccentric laws,
> The thoughtful soul this general influence draws,
> That an effect must presuppose a cause:
> And while she does her upward flight sustain,
> Touching each link of the continued chain,
> At length she is oblig'd and forc'd to see
> A first, a source, a life, a deity;
> What has forever been, and must forever be.

In 1732 Richard Gambol began his long poem *The Beauties of the Universe* with the lines

When universal nature I survey,
And mark eternal wisdom's bright display,
Where all is beauteous, all is wisely wrought,
Surpassing far the reach of humane thought:

Fully convinc'd, that God in all things shines,
Assenting reason straight my soul inclines
To love, adore, and that great Being praise,
Who did from nothing this fair structure raise.

With new knowledge emerging in biology, physico-theology expanded into natural theology. In 1802, William Paley, Archdeacon of Carlisle, authored a book on that subject. My reading was in the 1829 American edition of that book. Its title page bears the full message: *NATURAL THEOLOGY or Evidence of the Existence and Attributes of the DEITY Collected from the Appearances of Nature.*

Paley begins with the thought "Suppose I found a watch on the ground." He argues that the watch, because it is so admirably designed for a purpose, must have had a maker. In his words:

> The inference, we think, is inevitable; that the watch must have had a maker; that there must have existed, at some time and at some place or other, an artificer or artificers, who formed it for the purpose which we find it actually to answer; who comprehended its construction, and designed its use.

There cannot be design without a designer.

This line of reasoning has become known, using Paley's words, as the argument from design. After presenting the argument in exhausting detail Paley goes on to document the design of mechanical parts of organisms, the human frame, muscles, blood vessels, special structures, the relation of organisms to environment, insects, plants, the physical world, and the solar system.

The argument from design goes back to Aristotle's unmoved mover but required the scientific advances of the seventeenth and eighteenth centuries to come to its full fruition. The period of the preeminence of natural theology was short-lived. The reason is not hard to discern. The scholars who produced the elaborate evidences for design were almost universally clerics of the Church of England. They chose not to focus on the vast differences between the god of natural theology and the revealed God of Western religion.

The period from 1820 to 1860 witnessed the emergence of the new geology and the new biology. The earth was not six thousand years old; it was vastly older. Plants and animals were not mysteriously created in a few days; they evolved over millions of years. These contradictions to the Genesis narrative came from hard experimental evidence—indeed, rock-hard pieces of data.

Then came Darwin's *Origin of Species* and the great conflicts between science and organized religion. The clerics abandoned the argument from design; it was embedded in the same system of thought that was currently challenging their faith. Scientists abandoned the argument from design because it had come out of the same theological system that was now trying to deny to science the freedom to intepret the world in the light of experimental findings. The argument from design lay fallow for fifty years. Old Testament readers might say that design was awaiting its Jubilee.

In the early 1900s, Lawrence J. Henderson revived the argument from design within his perceptive work *The Fitness of the Environment*. He did not actually talk about design; rather, he noted:

> There is, however, one scientific conclusion which I wish to put forward as a positive and, I trust, fruitful outcome of the present investigation. The properties of matter and the course of cosmic evolution are now seen to be intimately related to the structure of the living being and to its activities; they become, therefore, far more important in biology than has been previously suspected. For the whole evolutionary process, both cosmic and organic, is one, and the biologist may now rightly regard the universe in its very essence as biocentric.

That statement did not overwhelm the scientific community, and Henderson is remembered rather ironically for the Henderson-Hasselbach equation, which relates the pH of a buffered solution to the amount of acid and salt present.

In any case, design was back in the arena and periodically appeared in the writings of aging scientists, who, freed from the idylls of the marketplace, could state their philosophical views without fear of peer pressure.

In 1979 Freeman Dyson attacked head-on a reexamination of design in light of the science of our time. His brief essay on theology occurs within a book appropriately titled *Disturbing the Universe*. Dyson is a prominent physicist and astrophysicist, and I think it came as a surprise to the scientific community when his book contained a chapter entitled "The Argument from Design."

He points out that many of the pre-Darwinian discussions of design focused on the biological world and the functional perfection of living structures. But this is precisely the area in which fitness and survival serve best to explain the world, so that when Thomas Huxley went out to do battle with the natural theologians, he had a ready-made and easy target. This path eventually led to the already discussed philosophical excesses of Jacques Monod's *Chance and Necessity*. Dyson takes on Monod much as I have in an earlier chapter. I would like to quote a paragraph of his thoughts:

> Jacques Monod has a word for people who think as I do and for whom he reserves his deepest scorn. He calls us "animists," believers in spirits. "Animism," he says, "established a covenant between nature and man, a profound alliance outside of which seems to stretch only terrifying solitude. Must we break this tie because the postulate of objectivity requires it?" Monod answers yes: "This ancient covenant is in pieces; man knows at last that he is alone in the universe's unfeeling immensity, out of which he emerged only by chance." I answer no. I believe in the covenant. It is true that we emerged in the universe by chance, but the idea of chance is itself only a cover for our ignorance. I do not feel like an alien in this

universe. The more I examine the universe and study the details of its architecture, the more evidence I find that the universe in some sense must have known that we were coming.

Dyson points to the role of mind in the domain of physics. He notes that there is just the right balance between the attractiveness of nuclear forces and the repulsion of the like charges of nucleons. If the repulsive forces were larger, nuclei could not exist. If the attractive forces were greater, all the protons of the universe would have been tied up in diprotons and all the hydrogen reactions that fuel the nuclear chemistry of the universe could not have taken place.

The actual fusion reactions of hydrogen in the sun depend on what physicists call the weak interaction. It controls the rate of fusion: much stronger and the stars would burn up too fast, much slower and they would be too cold.

Dyson goes on to point out that organic chemistry (and by extension biochemistry) depends on a delicate balance between electrical and quantum mechanical forces that come about because of the exclusion principle.

The thrust of Dyson's approach is very much in the mode of Henderson's, except that he adds mind, the immanent mind quality of the universe, as a further feature of design.

In the preceding chapters we, too, have looked at the workings of the biological and geological universes and have been impressed with how well the microscopic and macroscopic aspects come together. Like Dyson and Henderson and Teilhard, I find it hard not to see design in a universe that works so well. Each new scientific discovery seems to reinforce that vision of design. As I like to say to my friends, the universe works much better than we have any right to expect.

CHAPTER 20

Credo of a Mystical Scientist

My spiritual voyage through the universe is approaching an end, as is my sabbatical. The time has come to conclude this log, most of which has been written in the cabin of the yacht *The Good Guys*. This final entry begins with a trip ashore, and yet one last story.

One day a while back I was on the big island of Hawaii hiking in Volcanoes National Park. On the lower slopes of Mauna Loa is a kipuka, an island of life that remains when a river of molten lava splits into two streams that then rejoin. A kipuka is a rather interesting naturally formed ecological laboratory for studying a biological system in isolation from its terrestrial surroundings.

The large kipuka in the park has a nature trail rich in rather unusual flora and fauna that illustrate and illuminate many principles of microecology. On this trip I was planning to spend the entire day wandering through the park communing with nature in Thoreauvian fashion. It was early in the morning and the empty parking lot indicated that the territory was entirely mine for a short while.

With a printed guide to the nature trail in hand, I wandered through the kipuka. The sky was cloudless, the temperature was ideal, and birds were singing. It was a brief moment of insight, of idyllic communing with nature, and then—a large bee pierced my yellow Lahaina Yacht Club T-shirt and bit me on the left side in the soft flesh just above the belt line. In most un-Buddhist fashion, I slaughtered the offending beast, walked two steps forward, tripped on a rock, and fell, banging up my left knee on a nearby stone.

Lying on the ground with considerable pain in both side and knee, I had a second moment of insight. The cosmic grandeur of the universe does not spare us from local pain. The same design that has resulted in this gorgeous kipuka was also responsible for the bee that was following the law of an immanent god. The same force of gravity that holds the universe together was also involved in my falling in the middle of the kipuka. The universe is a strange mixture of cosmic joy and local pain. Within five seconds I had experienced both.

I did not spend a long period lying on the ground meditating. I have an uncertain allergy to the bites of various hymenoptera and I wondered if the slain attacker had colleagues with the same longing for human flesh. I limped back to the car, took some antihistamine from the first-aid kit, and sat in contemplation.

That experience does sum up for me some powerful facts about the universe. We do live in a world of cosmic joy. In thinking about the geospheres, I recorded in these pages the wondrous facts about the design of the universe and the interrelatedness of all parts. It is not possible to separate the workings of any one geosphere from the operations of the other three. Science alone leads us to the powerful realization that life is not an isolated property of some component of our planet but is an integrated aspect of the entire globe. No one thing is alive save for the fact that it is a temporary center of activity on a continuously animated stellar satellite. Each of us is a small part of a living whole existing in a vast universe whose design is wondrously oriented toward stars, planets, life, thought, and perhaps something more.

And so one sees, within the workings of the universe as revealed by science, a plan or cosmic intelligence that somehow had us in mind, not likely as individuals but as part of the evolving world of thought, the noosphere. To further know god's mind is to go back to science, to creative thought, and to further probe the laws of the universe.

The divine gifts are life and thought. The first challenge before us is to use those gifts to understand the giver or the universe of the gifts. That is religion. But what then of the local pain?

Pain and suffering are omnipresent. I accept the observation of Guatama Buddha that pain, suffering, and death are part of every life. But I do not accept his conclusion that we must submit passively to these affronts to human existence and merely seek surcease in a life designed to remove the desires that are the source of pain. Pain and suffering are inherent in design, but with the emergence of reflective thought, of the human mind, we are no longer totally enslaved to them but may participate in their alleviation. When mind turned back on itself in reflective thought, we became partners with god in making the future. Rather than being inexorably tied to pain and suffering, we are now free to devote ourselves to easing them and in some cases to conquering them.

What is so significant about the emergence of mind and the development of the noosphere is the fact that we are now involved and responsible, having the power within us to move the local world toward more cosmic joy and less local pain. If religion is the study of god's universe of cosmic joy, so ethics consists of good works to alleviate local pain.

And how are we to know good works? The same gifts of life and mind that enable us to explore the nature of the world also enable us to pursue a reasoned code of behavior. Just as science can be established by ratiocination, so can we seek behavioral norms by experience and reason. The fact that the ethical contents of all the world's religious systems have so much in common strongly suggests the possibility of a universal ethics in the same sense that we have a universal science. And just as our natural philosophy is tentative and paradigms change with new knowledge and new technology, so should we expect our moral codes to have the same dynamic character.

I would argue with those who concentrate just on pain and suffering. To do so is to deny cosmic joy, to deny the miracle of existence. This seems like an act of blasphemy.

I would equally confront those who spend their lives in paeans to cosmic wonderment and ignore the reality of pain and suffering. To do so seems like an act of nonconcern and selfishness. Individuals cannot save themselves; salvation is an act of planetary togetherness.

Between experiencing cosmic joy and alleviating local pain there is a path that each can follow. If it is a narrow path, it is at least wide enough to walk on, just like the finger pier I am now about to traverse, beginning the return from cosmic concerns to the responsibilities ahead.

Bibliography

Bergson, Henri. *Creative Evolution.* New York: Random House, Inc., 1944.

Continents Adrift and Continents Aground: Readings from Scientific American. San Francisco: W. H. Freeman and Company, 1976.

Darwin, Charles. *On the Origin of Species by Means of Natural Selection, or the Preservation of Favoured Races in the Struggle for Life.* 1859.

Dyson, Freeman. *Disturbing the Universe.* New York: Harper and Row, 1979.

Henderson, Lawrence J. *The Fitness of the Environment.* Boston: Beacon Press, 1959.

Lovelock, J. E. *Gaia: A New Look at Life on Earth.* New York: Oxford University Press, 1979.

Margenau, Henry. *The Nature of Physical Reality.* Woodbridge, Conn.: Ox Bow Press, 1977.

McKean, Richard. *The Philosophy of Spinoza.* New York: Longmans, Green and Company, 1928.

Monod, Jacques. *Chance and Necessity.* New York: Alfred A. Knopf, 1971.

Morowitz, H. J., and L. S. Morowitz. *Life on the Planet Earth.* New York: W. W. Norton and Co., 1974.

BIBLIOGRAPHY

Morowitz, Harold. *Energy Flow in Biology.* Woodbridge, Conn.: Ox Bow Press, 1979.

Morris, Henry M. *The Troubled Waters of Evolution.* San Diego: Creation-Life, 1975.

Northrop, F. S. C. *The Logic of the Sciences and the Humanities.* Woodbridge, Conn.: Ox Bow Press, 1983.

Rankama, K., and T. G. Sahama. *Geochemistry.* Chicago: University of Chicago Press, 1952.

Sagan, Carl, and I. S. Shklovskii. *Intelligent Life in the Universe.* San Francisco: Holden Day, 1966.

Spinoza, Baruch. *The Philosophy of Spinoza.* Introduction by Joseph Ratner. New York: Random House, 1927.

Stanley, Steven M. *The New Evolutionary Time Table.* New York: Basic Books, Inc., 1981.

Teilhard de Chardin, Pierre. *The Phenomenon of Man.* New York: Harper and Row, 1959.

Thoreau, Henry David. *Walden, or, Life in the Woods.* 1854.

Turekian, Karl K. *Oceans.* Englewood Cliffs, N.J.: Prentice Hall, 1968.

Weinberg, Steven. *The First Three Minutes.* New York: Basic Books, 1976.

Index

Index

About the Author

HAROLD J. MOROWITZ is professor of molecular biophysics and biochemistry at Yale University. He is the author of *The Wine of Life* and *Mayonnaise and the Origin of Life*. He lives in New Haven, Connecticut.